A Touch of Saccharine

Edited by: A.J. Huffman
and April Salzano

Cover Art: "Sweets Candies" stock photo from public domain
http://www.pdpics.com/photo/2047-sweets-candies/

Copyright © 2014 A.J. Huffman

All rights reserved. Except for brief quotations in critical articles or reviews, no part of this book may be reproduced in any manner without prior written permission from the publisher:

Kind of a Hurricane Press
www.kindofahurricanepress.com
kindofahurricanepress@yahoo.com

CONTENTS

April Salzano	*We Are What We Eat . . .*	3

From the Authors

Allen Ashley	*Sweet the Sin*	7
Barbara Bald	*Sweet Reunion*	8
James Bell	*Vending Machine*	9
Andrew Campbell-Kearsey	*Sweet Boy*	10
Theresa A. Cancro	*Jawbreaker*	13
J.R. Carson	*Homemade Sugars*	14
Alan Catlin	*Candy*	15
Cathleen Chambless	*Going Steady in 2013*	16
Oliver Cutshaw	*Jesus and the Chocolate Bars: A Parable*	17
Joseph M. Faria	*The 4th of July Parade*	18
Pattie Flint	*Talk to Me in Marzipan*	19
Chris Fradkin	*The First Time That I Tried It*	20
Phil Ginsburg	*Assorted Centers*	21
Jessica Gleason	*Acid Reflux*	22
John Grochalski	*Surveillance State*	23
	Some Days are Like Wrestling with Hell	25

Lynn-Marie Harper	Candy-Striped Dresses	27
William Ogden Haynes	Expatriate Games	29
Art Heifetz	Sweets and Coffee	30
Ruth Holzer	Sweets	31
Liz Hufford	The Candy That Can't Be Named	32
S.E. Ingraham	Solace Found in Sugar	34
	Pink Sweetness	35
Diane Jackman	Mrs. Lester's Sweet Shop	37
Leland James	Hard Candy	38
Judith Janoo	Sweet Elegy	39
Mark Allen Jenkins	Altoids	41
Joyce Kessel	A Tea Quartet	42
Marla Kessler	The Job Interview	44
Steve Klepetar	Candy Tree	46
	Eye Candy	47
Mark M. Lewis	Candy Man	48
Deborah R. Majors	Temporary Duty	51
Jacqueline Markowski	Submerged	54
Grace Maselli	Frying Pan Road	57
	We'd Love to Come but We Have Dietary Restrictions	58

Shirley McClure	*Shipwrecked*	59
Catfish McDaris	*Working Like a Fool*	60
	The Wrong Place	61
Ron McFarland	*Ode to Chocolate*	62
Matt McGee	*I (Still) Want Candy*	64
	The Traders	65
Joan McNerney	*How Sweet!*	66
Karla Linn Merrifield	*Gamed-Out*	67
	You Burn Me	68
	Childhood Chocolates	69
James B. Nicola	*Three Poets*	70
Cristina M. R. Norcross	*Just One Chocolate, Slowly*	71
	Death By Turtle	72
George H. Northrup	*Cookies for Breakfast*	74
Vincent O'Connor	*First Kiss*	75
Susan Oke	*Too Sweet*	76
Carl Palmer	*Easter Egg Hunt*	78
Mangal Patel	*Mischief Moments*	79
Richard King Perkins II	*Cocoa Shadows and Chocolate Cosmos*	82
	Lines of Lost Chocolate	83
David Pointer	*Candy-Gram on Wheels*	84

Stephen V. Ramey	Leaf Licker	85
Edward J. Rielly	Our Mounds Candy Bar	87
Zack Rogow	Sweet Tooth	88
Brad Rose	Narrow Escape from a Near Miss	90
	Old Dirk Savors the Prospect of Honeymoon Bliss with His Second Teen Bride	91
	Pink Candy Hearts	92
	It's for Me, Cupid	93
Janice D. Rubin	Campbell River	94
Len Saculla	Sweet Sting	96
Bobbi Sinha-Morey	The Last Days	99
	Missing	100
Smita Sriwastav	Candied Snippets of Nature . . .	101
	Candy Foil Memories . . .	103
	The Kick of Eclairs	104
Marianne Szlyk	My Mother Told Stories	106
	On Gray Thursdays	108
	The Poet Dances with Inanimate Object	110
Yermiyahu Ahron Taub	Diabetic's Fantasia	112
	Candy Tattoo	113
David Turnbull	I Want Candy	115

Annaliese Wagner	*A Tourist in India*	117
Mercedes Webb-Pullman	*Lunch with My Mother and Her Friends*	118
	Choosing Memories Like Chocolate	120
Joanna M. Weston	*Getting Acquainted*	122
Ron Yazinski	*Placebo*	123
Jennifer Zidon	*Retiring*	125

From the Editors

A.J. Huffman	*I Segregate My Jellybeans*	129
	Gummy Bear Sex Ends with ER Visit	130
	Life is *Like a Box of Chocolates*	131
	With Slice	132
	I Would Kill to Lick a Tic Tac	133
	Two Jelly	134
	With Lollipop	135
April Salzano	*Finding the Center*	136
	Beggar's Booty	137
	(Lemon)Heads are Gonna Roll	138
	Peanut Butter Meltaway	139
	Whatchamacallit	140
	Fear is	141
	How Many Licks Does it Take	142

Author Bios	145
About the Editors	161

We Are What We Eat…

…or as these poems shows us, we are also what we think about eating, what we remember eating, what we wish we could eat, and what we refuse to eat. Candy, specifically, has a certain power over us, it seems. It brings about a nostalgia and reverence for the carefree days of childhood when we did not have to count calories or worry about overindulging. It was our magic potion before coffee and energy drinks, before responsibilities and regret. Candy calls to mind memories, symbolized by confections no longer created—candy cigarettes, extinct varieties of chocolate, licorices that cannot be named. We remember our loved ones by the favorite chocolate they ate and shared with us, or hid, or gave as gifts. For some of us, candy serves as a comfort food in all its delicious forms. For others, candy means danger and forbidden longing.

Candy is its own kind of poetry, so easily making the transfer into metaphor. The "pieces" in this collection take shape into an assortment of flavors so varied in tone and interpretation of the theme we selected that readers will need to digest them slowly, one at a time, as we did. Some of the poems and stories can be sucked on like hardtack, with sweetness that will linger long after completion. Others will be devoured quickly, bitten straight through. Some go well with coffee in the morning, others as a late night snack. Some are layered, coated in a sweetness that disguises a thick center, others are made of a more transparent sugar, but just as sticky. All of them, however, will leave you wanting more.

From The Authors

Sweet the Sin

Welcome to the body's battlefield
between taste and texture.
Casualties and collateral are mounting.

The tongue craves sweetness,
primary amongst its flavour pointers.
Some of us have little time or inclination
for salty or sour.
The yawning hole in my belly –
briefly filled with a sugar rush –
is paralleled by dental cavities.
Every sucked barley sugar,
every mouthful of dissolving candy floss
– a sticky cloud on a stick –
every comforting liquorice allsort
or iced cake half-made with sweet,
sweet desiccated coconut –
these have been the cravings
that have scraped off the enamel
whilst piling on the calories.
Just the way it goes.

The pink and white cylinder of
        seaside rock
used to have " Blackpool " or "Southend"
written all the way through it.
Now it carries a Government Health Warning,
with the picture of beach and pier
replaced by fine words and a gappy
        scientific diagram.
No one's fooled;
especially not the endorphins.
Snap. Crunch. Check the composition
of those candy shards.

                -- Allen Ashley

Sweet Reunion

You could buy penny candy in a soda shop when I was a kid.
Bubble gum cigarettes poised between your forefinger and thumb,
pinky held high in the air, you could puff with the best of them.
Wax lips in brilliant red could turn you into a clown,
movie star or harlot (if you knew what that was).

There were licorice-filled, pink and white Good and Plenty,
Necco wafers that looked like pastel-colored poker chips,
Ju-Ju Bees that stuck to your braces, and yes,
wax bottles you could suck sticky colored syrup out of,
then chew wad-like in your mouth.

A thumb could dispense Pez pieces, small rectangular delicacies
from plastic mouths of bears, pirates, King Kong and Howdy Doody.
We'd offer these simulated tongues to friends like Bobby Dunn
who limped when he struck out at a game, gave them
to teachers like Mr. Martin who tutored us through tough math quizzes,
extended them even to grandma when her white hair
came out a little too blue.

Fifty years later in a world bend on fluoride toothpaste,
whitening strips, mouth-freshening mints and dental floss,
thoughts of these candies still join those who, some long gone,
shared in the sugary gift. Linking memory to memory
and faces to places, they continue to stir sweetness
that resists the grave.

-- Barbara Bald

Vending Machine

through the glass I see
how chocolate bars
take up the top two rows -
for eighty or ninety cents
have the furthest to fall
when I put the money in
to snicker when my Snickers
make a long prat fall
or my Kit-Kat cracks with a yeowl
as it hits the bin below -
third down are the sandwiches
that might scrunch in their plastic
if placed any higher - bottled water
next would bob and burble
bounce a little in the bin -
cans are on the bottom row
because of the dent potential -
so chocolate bars have furthest
to fall - have no choice in the matter -
decide M&Ms will have the softest landing
and pay ninety cents for proof

-- James Bell

Sweet Boy

Tony's a sweet boy. Says he's thirty-three but he looks younger to me. Probably trying to impress me by how grownup he is. My neighbour Renie was a bit suspicious at first. 'He's after your money and make sure you hide your decent jewellery'. As if I have much of either! I always reckoned she was jealous that we bought our council flat.

Tony's very polite. Always calls me Mrs Thomas. I tried to get him to call me Elsie. Tony started began shopping and changing library books. Now he fixes the odd thing around the flat. I didn't mind giving him keys, as he pops in at all hours and he seems as honest as the day's long.

I don't think he's after anything physical. Just as well at my age. He calls me 'love' and 'dear'. More than my husband ever did. I did worry that Tony would want to move in, but it's never come up. Best that we live separately.

My neck's all stiff and my joints are playing up again. Fell asleep in the chair last night. I tell Tony, 'Don't grow old'. He just smiles. He's a man of few words but he writes a lot, never goes anywhere without his notebook. Here's Renie now. I never have any other visitors and Tony has his own key.

"Just checking you're still alive, Else. Has your young man been round yet?"

"No, but I expect he'll be here presently. Something different about you Renie?"

I know perfectly well she's had her hair dyed but quite why a woman of our age would want to have her hair the colour of a pillar box defeats me.

She touched the back of her head and says, "Do you like it?"

"Well it'll certainly get you noticed."

*****

Back in my living room I sit down to do the crossword. Tony suggested I do them. But the paper's nowhere to be found. I make a cup of tea. There's my paper, in the fridge next to the milk. I reckon I've got a poltergeist or something. Happening a lot recently, things going missing or ending up in funny places.

I've been sleeping a lot in the day. Tony reckons I need one of those armadillos. No that's not right? Armbands? No, it'll come to me in a minute. An alarm clock to wake me after a nap. I hear his key in the lock, no time for a bit of face powder.

"Can I come in, Mrs Thomas? Are you decent?"

'Cheeky sod!' I think but I just laugh when he comes in.

"I see you've got a cup of tea."

I touch the china. Stone cold. I must have dozed off again. At least I'm clear of the headache today.

"I just need a bit of shopping, Tony. The usual please. Do you want me to write it down for you?"

"I know what to get. Are you running low on biscuits?"

I never eat the things. I only get them in for him and Renie. Couple of gannets they are. I normally get him a bar of chocolate. He's got quite a sweet tooth, I've discovered.

*****

Tony will be back soon. First time he's left his notepad. I know I shouldn't, but it won't harm to take a peek. Wonder if it's poems.

*****

That was a shock. He's paid by the local authority to be my carer. He even had the cheek to ask Renie to keep an eye on me. Apparently I've got vascular dementia. I'm his case study for his course at the university.

He won't be getting any more Hobnobs off me.

-- Andrew Campbell-Kearsey

Jawbreaker

Givin' you my most
luscious smile, a bit of eye candy,
to lure you over,
since you seem to
prey on the weak,
on the small, on the mellow people.

See you take the bait, lick those
dry, crooked lips, cool lascivious look
(but you won't crush me, ever).
I got somethin' for you,
right here.

Come closer...Pow!
Yeah, jawbreaker.

Not from the gum machine.

-- Theresa A. Cancro

Homemade Sugars

Ingredients:

4,000 candy bars	72,000 gallons of sweet tea
12,480 cans of soda	2,600 pounds of pasta
6,240 dinner rolls	3,000 missed gym appointments
2,080 slices of cake	3 years of regret

Directions:

1. In a large pan of self-pity, add all ingredients and stir over high stress for at least twenty years.
2. Periodically add guilt to taste.
3. In the final year of cooking, add two toes and the sight in one eye.
4. Serve warm, with a dollop of surprise mixed with one half teaspoon of acceptance.

Original recipe yields 250 pounds of flesh.

Serves: 1

-- J.R. Carson

Candy

I eat caramel candy apples
in the Coney Island night

mother holds the cold steel
railing watching the sky splitting

rides fall through the garish
lights she says smells like

the burnt butter and stale popcorn
places she hides the soft used

gummed candies of her dreams

-- Alan Catlin

Going Steady in 2013

You tell me
we're Allison & Cry-Baby,
because I'm your square,
with cherry lips,
you're my grease,
hand cuffs released-
diatonic to each other's keys,
Lucille to BB King.
We hook up
King Khan & BBQ Show,
phone to car stereo,
shoes shuffle against gravel,
silhouettes silk screened to headlights,
bodies pressed,
fret & strings,
sway with melodies & palm trees,
"No Outlet" sign & salty waves,
our own lover's lane.
The scythe moon
reflects in your sun
glasses & they slightly slide
down your nose, passing
off the night
sky to your eyes,
microdot sprinkles
on Snow Caps,
you kiss me with lips
like pink Sweet Tart
candy hearts,
XOXO,
we part & I press
my cheek against
your chest & cry, its
too much Rock N' Roll
for me to handle.

-- Cathleen Chambless

Jesus and the Chocolate Bars: A Parable

After the stiffness of worship,
in the brick and brown of church,
drowsy from the silence of serious songs,
we are herded single file into the basement
for another hour of cleansing.
Reciting the platitudes, recalling the Apostles,
staring solemnly at our Sunday School teacher,
we are stuffed with the glory of scripture,
but the only word we hunger for is chocolate.
Finally we are set free, rush up the stairs
and slam out the door,
just a block down to the Candy store.
We are anxious legs, and greedy mouths,
we pull the handle and the little bell rings,
sweet rolls on one side and over here bubble gum,
lollipops and licorice lying in rows.
The dimes and quarters roll out of our pockets,
we should have given them to the collection plate,
but sweet, sour, and sugary tempted us.
We fidgeted through all that hush and bother, for this moment,
biting into a bar, peanut and caramel strings twisting from our mouths.
A guilty, guileless pleasure.

-- Oliver Cutshaw

The 4th of July Parade

Rockets blare.
    She sleeps.
    The clowns hand out balloons.
    She sleeps.
    A parade of soldiers salute.
    She sleeps.
    Your mother is sitting in a lawn chair with her head tilting toward the sun. You're wearing blue shorts and a red and white polo, holding the arm of the chair. You're frightened by the clown who is handing you a bag of hard candy.
    "Take the candy, kid," the clown says.
    Batons whirl and girls cartwheel.
    She sleeps.
    Applause for the Mayor.
    She sleeps.
    You eclipse the sun. Your mother wakes, startled by the shade of you standing in front of her. You hold a torn paper bag of candy.
    She lifts a hand to wipe away the tiny tears.
    "Aren't you enjoying the parade, sweetie?" she says.

-- Joseph M. Faria

Talk to Me in Marzipan

I want to be covered in
smooth pink. roll up
little balls and cut them
up four ways I'll bloom
bleeding and sugary
monuments sprout
frozen in refrigerated
slices and crumbling
stained saints. spin me
on wooden sticks, paint
me in petaled lapels
pink and rubbed red.

-- Pattie Flint

The First Time That I Tried It

It
melted
in
my
mouth.

I
tossed
it
back
and
forth.

I
closed
my
eyes.

The
nectar
flowed
like
honey.

And so I had my first chocolate cherry.

-- Chris Fradkin

Assorted Centers

As a teenager I remember coming home after a night out with my friends
The police would be parked in front of my house

My parents had been fighting again and someone called the cops
Sometimes there would be an empty box of candy strewn all over the lawn

My father's attempts at reconciliation had ended with nougats in the hedges
Butter creams in the magnolias
Dark chocolate caramels decomposing among the perennials

I once found two milk chocolate marshmallows
Still in there brown paper swaddling clothes
Huddled together like a pair of runaways from a Fanny Farmer foster home

Our house had only one center
It was always nuts

Just nuts.

-- Phil Ginsburg

Acid Reflux

Even though I know,
really know,
that I'll be doubled-over
regretful
afterwards.

I still shovel the
chocolate
into my greedy
mouth.

Not bothering to take it
slow
I swallow
until all that's left
is a lonely
wrapper
and the sting
of bloated
instant
regret.

-- Jessica Gleason

Surveillance State

she comes up to me
with her prune face and shitty james patterson novel

i want you to check the surveillance tape, she says
pointing at the security camera that's always aimed at me

why? i ask

because some kid spilled candy outside
and i stepped in it

lady, last week some kid got stabbed on this block

she rolls her eyes at this

what's a little stabbing
when there's jujubes scattered all over the pavement?

jesus christ, she says
well can't you do anything?
i mean someone needs to get this kid
and teach him a lesson about decency and respect

mam, last month the bodega across the street
get held up at gunpoint

so? she says

nothing, i say

then we stand there looking at the video screen
as it flashes the interior and exterior of the building
as it shows us around the corner and down the block
the front entrance with the smallest trace of candy littered about

see? see? she shouts
like she's just caught bin laden or dillinger in the act
there it is! there it is! evidence!

get the surveillance tape, she shouts
to whoever will listen

while i grab a broom and a dustpan
and head out into the horrible heat of the day
to clean up the crime scene

forgetting to tell her that back in january
two girls were mugged and almost raped in this neighborhood

but what would it matter to her
without there being even one
snickers bar wrapper at the crime scene?

-- John Grochalski

Some Days are Like Wrestling with Hell

i stand in the pharmacy line
waiting to buy nasal spray
with all of the other sick fools
holding their bottles of medicine

everyone seems to be coughing or sneezing
and there is no end in sight to this line

the woman at the front of it
is shaking a flier and arguing the sale price
on a family pack of paper towels

in front of me is some old bat
buying the mother lode of junior mints
because they are on special this week

she is talking to two loud children
who are wearing snowcaps that look like animals
they won't stop shouting about school or one thing or another

they touch every candy bar and pack of gum
knocking them on the floor
as the store manager smiles, nods,
and picks up after them

their mother is buying an assortment of shit
that no one needs

none of them are paying attention to the line
to the cashier standing there screaming, next!

so i go
which causes an uproar the second i step out of line

the little animal headed girls shout
their mother whines

the old bat with the junior mints
tells everyone that she didn't know that the line was moving

the cashier gives me a look like i'm the devil
but all i want is to have normal sinus passages
to not get cancer from my base desire to breathe properly

so i tell them all, fuck it
it's your world and i just live in it, right?

i re-take my place back in line
thinking that some days are like wrestling with hell
for the simplest of things

as the mother with the animal headed children
steps up to pay for all of her shit

and the old bat with the junior mints
turns to look at me and says

aren't those two little girls just darling?

-- John Grochalski

Candy-Striped Dresses

Candy-striped dresses,
Three blue and white
Different styles
A woman and two girls
Different ages.

They posed in front of a wall
The woman sat
The girls stood
The photograph hung on the
Older girl's hallway wall

The younger one's heart and memory.

It was on a slide in the drawer
And though they were 62 and 58
The light that lit it was the same, yesterday today and tomorrow.

Neither could remember where it was taken
Or by whom
The railings above the wall
Gave leeway to think Zoo
But it could've been anywhere.

One day the older one
Became aware
That just as their mother
Had passed into the ever present light
Then so one day would her sister
The little girl with a short fringe

And so would she
the older one with plaits.

She had forgotten what candy-striped meant
Until that moment
With the brainstorm list in front of her

Candy was pink, like Blackpool Rock
With the words swathed through
Glazed with sugar

Sugar, sweet, candy for the tongue
Candy-striped was blue and white, an image

A feast for the memory.

-- Lynn-Marie Harper

Expatriate Games

None of us knew why, but
there was only one place in
our part of Japan for Air Force
brats to get Tootsie Roll pops.
So, we rode a series of trains and
busses for hours to the store at the
Naval base in Yokohama thinking
of ourselves as smugglers
and astute men of business.
We bought them by the box
for two cents apiece to sell
back up north for a nickel
to other high school boys.
But we would give them away for free
to the girls before asking them out
on a steamy date at the teen club or base theater.
On the trip back from Yokohama, we rode the train
like kings, a head taller than the Japanese,
looking down at a sea of black hair
extending the entire length of the car.
The white cardboard sticks protruded from
our mouths at jaunty angles like cigars
as we sucked on the candy tasting of
lemons, cherries, and grapes.
And the longer we sucked the pops,
the candy shell became progressively thinner.
Most of us were tempted to bite through,
but true connoisseurs waited until the last
moment to do so, because hitting that
Tootsie Roll center was tantamount to an orgasm.
Those were the years we were boy-men in Japan,
American contradictions with suckers
in our mouths and Trojans in our wallets.

-- William Ogden Haynes

Sweets and Coffee

We brush off the flour
by tapping the pieces against
the side of the box.
And clump by clump,
we savor the chewy dough,
the small bits of pistachio
clinging to the roofs of our mouths.

The most sublime of candies,
according to our guest,
shoots from the hole
between an insect's legs,
to be collected sweet and sticky
from a plant in north Iraq.
Al mann, Iraqis call it,
after the white substance
which fell from heaven
upon the wandering Jews.

The richest coffee in the world,
we tell our friend,
is grown in Bali,
the beans digested by a civet
and shat out in his cage
at seventy bucks a pot.

We sip it slowly
from a china demi-tasse
just to get our money's worth.
We take another piece of *mann*.
We marvel that the most exalted tastes
should come from such a lowly place.

-- Art Heifetz

Sweets

Cheap cinema seats and Kit Kat bars,
milk chocolates, nut-filled, melting,
smeared on the tatty velveteen. Feet up
for an intermission smoke. Red licorice,
smooth butterscotch at story's end.
And then the rush to flee *God Save the Queen*.

That was the Gate at Notting Hill.
Its grainy films, a sort of life.
Around the corner, up the road,
I'd hurry back to Ladbroke Grove,
lacking threepence for the bus
and stuffed with sweets to a fare-thee-well.
Darkened cabs would crawl the curb,
offering me free rides to anywhere.

-- Ruth Holzer

The Candy That Can't Be Named

Can you be a racist at three,
not knowing there are races?
I sounded like one,
placing my order at the corner store,
a doll and a candy for a penny.

I'd play with them first,
make them dance or sing,
until my fingers melted sugar
and stuck together.
Time to bite,
the insides smooth and shiny
like tar bubbles in summer heat.

In the sweet, raucous sixties
the candy disappeared with childhood.
Perhaps they remade themselves,
like Cassius Clay became Ali.
Licorice babies.

In college I met my first coloreds,
later African-Americans,
then Blacks.
A lone Panther prowled my campus,
turned up in sociology classes,
seemed a bit grumpy.
From the safe distance of television,
I crushed on Bobby Seale.

On my first job at a rural campus,
recruited minorities wandered
like lost tribes, searching for cosmetics
and foods our stores didn't carry.
At night I studied Black English:
"The eagle flies on Friday night."
Classes were held in the Tower of Babel.

Then Larry and Ann stepped out of the clamshell, rising.
Larry became a lawyer.
I saw Ann through the murder of her brother,
for dating a white girl.

And somewhere along the way I lost my taste for licorice.

-- Liz Hufford

Solace Found in Sugar

The weather gods are frowning outright
Threatening the city with chain lightning,
smatterings of chilly rain, and over all
There are clouds the colour of slate

It is a day for curling up with a good book
A fire blazing in the grate, and always by me
Sweets – all kinds of confectionary comfort

First, my love brings me white-chocolate-
raspberry cheesecake – two slices to savour
and partake of slowly – they are very dear:

Each piece costs over seven dollars! I do try
to make them last, not always successfully...
He knows this, so with kindness, he supplements

In addition to the cheesecake comes junk food:
Chocolate bars, M & M's, Hostess cupcakes
And, should my love feel the need to pamper
me further... there will be Godiva truffles too

More bits of decadence that don't bear
thinking about much when it comes
to price, but are rich beyond all measure.

Hmm – I find myself suddenly at the window
eyeing the now bright blue sky resentfully...

-- S.E. Ingraham

Pink Sweetness

She never could
resist cotton
candy; it was
the colour
of baby booties,
the ones her sister
had from her auntie
knitted specially
just for her

And it melted like snow
on her tongue,
only sweet
like sugar
that stuck
to her teeth
So when
the man offered
her a cloud
of candy
she just didn't
even think...

Sobbing
in the trunk
of his car,
she knew
it was
her fault
Everybody
knew not
to take candy
from a stranger
Not even
cotton candy

pink as
baby booties

        -- S.E. Ingraham

Mrs. Lester's Sweet Shop

Drowned as a witch for that sixth finger;
when villagers tilled the open fields,
that would have brought her early death.
Now she taps the stump to cast
a spell of kindness.

Five barley sugar twists glowing gold
in the slatted sunlight, five gobstoppers,
striped red and green, five flying saucers,
sugar mice, chocolate frogs, jumping jacks.
Always, always they ask for five.

The children think she doesn't notice,
tipping the sweets from wide-necked jars
into rustling paper cones,
counting on her deformed hand
so each receives an extra gift,
given with love for children never born.

-- Diane Jackman

Hard Candy

rock sky
    blood ice
doubt and grace
sandpaper tongue
  hard candy lace

hard candy can be
black
as midnight ice
black
as the widow's veil
  -- a pack of horehounds
    jaw-breaking bitter
licorice sticks and stones

    or bright as a parrot
      flavors untold
  red hot
      butterscotch
great balls of fire!

eyes close to the glass
  the light playing tricks
        landscapes
out of this world

ladies swirl in rainbow gowns
men in white suits and red ties
    bow in rows

wintergreen leaves
    bird eggs
      broken dreams
and birthday balloons

              -- Leland James

Sweet Elegy

Oh, glass jars of fireballs and gumballs,
taffy and root beer barrels, cinnamon swirls,
caramels, the wonderment,
a grocer's shelf discovered for a cent.

Visiting homes had its sweet greetings.
The woman who raised goats
bent over the stove
working the wooden spoon to thicken
brown-sugared cream into penuche.
The milk lady gave lemon drops when
we bought quarts of fresh Jersey.

At our home, hot fudge bubbling in a pot,
poured over dollops of vanilla
cream: behold maraschino cherry,
take your throne.
I still dream
of my hand in the black licorice bowl
kept above the kitchen cabinet, out of
reach, and I, reaching into it and caught—
the elder child trusted to form peanut butter
and coconut into fudge treats to offer our guests.

We part now, newly unsuitable confections. You
never lessened, only my view,
encased in a museum of sweetness.

No longer a child before the grocer's shelf,
no more licorice bowl high above me or
goat lady's penuche, no
gold-wrapped quarters for Christmas.
Eros dissolve like lemon drops.
Every form of chocolate now a lament:
dark, light, milky and white,

each chew; hard, sticky, twisted,
and pulled, lay to rest my taste for you.

And when you call I won't answer,
sweet longing without end.

-- Judith Janoo

Altoids

Like magnesium burning
my mouth down,
the sudden flare blasts
me down the interstate.

When my eyes blur
between brake lights and phosphorescent highway stripes, I make out
the white and red tin
between tan car seats, flip it open
like a cigarette pack
and thrust a few to my tongue.

The light from my lips,
a small spotlight, breaches
the dark path from Detroit.

       -- Mark Allen Jenkins

A Tea Quartet

1. Black Tea

it's what she grew up with
not knowing it was once currency
but it bonds her with generations of women
and keeps its flavor for years
like the laughter of memories
& the easy conversations of ancestors

2. Green Tea

the magazines all proclaim its health benefits
an asian mystic secret of antioxidants
or polyphenols
and other things she can't pronounce
or remember
all she knows is it can't be
the first cup of the day
and wonders how anything
that tastes this good can be so good for you
except dark chocolate

3. Oolong

she pours the water carefully
a ritual of tea leaves
preparing for a good long book
and a quiet night
the thrum of rain outside
and a snoring dog beside the chair
like a still life
a cliché of comfort
or an escape into magic

4. White Tea

the emperor's is the rarest
like waking from a dream
in the solitude of the quietest morning
and simply knowing
all is right with the world

-- Joyce Kessel

The Job Interview

I was about to retire, so I spent the last few months trying to find my replacement. The first batch of applicants was absolutely awful! I am not sure why kids today don't think they have to work for a living. In my day, we were grateful for any job.

I rewrote the advertisement to improve our candidate pool. We needed someone industrious, a self starter. He would have to be a problem solver since issues came up all the time. The intensity of our factory was extreme at times, so thinking under pressure was a "must have." We also needed a natural leader. I was a shift manager. We couldn't waste time with someone that would take too long to develop. Business training was a plus.

When my last candidate of the day came in, I immediately knew he wouldn't work out. He had a real attitude about high season. He said he didn't see the need to work overtime. I tried to explain that we were in the perishables business.

"You could smooth out demand over the year. Most of your products have a shelf life of 24 months. There is no reason not to pre-pack them."

It sounded like someone who hadn't been on the front line. We spent eleven months of the year accumulating those items. The last month was a combination of production and assembly. Everything was then delivered over a one-day period using thousands of couriers. We scheduled things to the minute.

"And where would we keep the baskets?"

"You could use the advanced storage system that they deploy up North. You collect used baskets in April and have them cleaned and ready to go in May. The baskets could be stacked with packing materials in place by July. And for goodness sakes, stop buying your candy in September and October! Everyone knows you are paying Halloween premiums."

Wow, he had a point. I had been thinking about that for years. But our schedule was developed long before Halloween went commercial. Back then, pagan rituals didn't even involve confectionary items. I was especially intrigued to hear that Santa was using this already. His operations were world-class.

"But what about the eggs? Painting them is a bottleneck. You can't freeze egg whites, so we always have to boil and decorate them at the last minute."

He smiled. He had already thought about it. "We are going to spray paint 50% of them and call it *graffiti eggs*. And the witches, who honestly have nothing to do before Halloween, have agreed to cast a spell over at least 25% of them to just make them look like they are decorated."

I wasn't sure how the Easter Bunny was going to react to all of this, but he only asked one question before hiring the kid. "After the witches do the eggs, is there any way they could make me look like Zac Efron?"

-- Marla Kessler

Candy Tree

In our yard, my father planted
a candy tree. It withered and died.
Next year a bush emerged from
red licorice roots, blossomed
with gumballs, jujubes and Dots.
We picked them in the fall,
our hands sticky and stained
like rainbows dipped in honey glaze.

He kept them in Mason jars.
At night I heard the red ones
shriek, yellows chuckle and cough,
felt the heavy silence of the greens.
We held the black ones back
for seed, anise root power spreading
through our shed, miasma of scent
among garden gloves and trowels.

-- Steve Klepetar

Eye Candy

They told me I was eye candy
and flossed me till my hair fell out

they told me I was sweet
and dumped me in a glass of lemonade

when they told me I was chocolate-smooth
and made a wax impression of my face

they shoved me on a stick
and licked me down to this sticky core

they planted me on a mountainside
of cake, they flipped me in the air

and swallowed me one by one
when they found me behind the easy chair

covered in dust and lint, I cursed them
in a language of teeth and burning breath

so they named me *gumdrop* and *sour ball*
they named me *lollipop* and *lemon drop*

they held me in their hands and whispered *mint*
then poked a hole right through the middle of my heart

-- *Steve Klepetar*

Candy Man

Since the accident, he wasn't sure if it was children or bugs he was more scared of. Adults viewed him with pity, sympathy, even revulsion, but both children and bugs saw him differently and both would follow wherever he should go. He was grateful for a cold Autumn day with a blank sky and gentle drizzle keeping children and bugs away, but looking over his shoulder, was that Ice Cream van there again?

If only he had emptied his pockets during the experiment. Dr B and his colleagues had learned from science fiction movies such as The Fly, that hygiene was of the utmost importance when conducting a teleportation experiment. Both the In and Out tubes had been carefully swept out and mosquito nets put up to ensure no small organisms would intrude. No-one reckoned on the problems that would be caused by the contents of Dr B's trouser pockets.

The experiment worked, in that Dr B disappeared from the In booth and reappeared in the Out booth. Unfortunately, he did not come out quite the same man as he went in. When his DNA had been scanned in the dematerialization process, a biochemical reaction had occurred with the Pick'n'Mix in the doctor's pockets.

There was much cheering as Dr B's form started to materialize in the Out tube, with the smoke adding to the sense of mystery and wonder. The cheers turned to silence, turned to screams as his image became clearer. All too clear.

His skin was too pale. Candy dentures had replaced his teeth and long strawberry strings taken over for hair. Worst of all, his Smartie eyes stared out of his soft face. Dr B was now a man of confectionery.

He took to wearing large floppy hats and veils, completely covering his sweet skin. His own Spaniel, Minty, had chewed off a candy ear in his sleep. On that first walk home, before he had started covering himself so as to be as airtight as possible, he was soon covered in wasps, bees and flies. His skin was pocked with hundreds of tiny bite marks when he reached home and these never healed. His brother's small children

had taken and eaten his left hand before their parents could stop them. Worst, however, were his new Smartie eyes. They were fixed, open and staring so his vision was stark and unblinking, except for when he fell asleep, when he dreamed confused nightmares about funfairs, theatres and factories. Since he had woken up to the horror of being eaten by ants, with one warrior ant scurrying away with one of his eyes, he had covered up fully for bedtime too, and wore goggles to safeguard his remaining eye. For cosmetic reasons he glued a new Smartie to replace his lost eye, but this one provided no vision.

All of the major confectionery companies made him sponsorship offers, several offered him greater riches if they could run taste tests on him. The most persistent of these was Chocolate and Ice Cream baron, Wacky Whalley.

In desperation, he saw a Harley Street doctor. He had to pay from his own diminishing funds as the insurance company defined his transformation as 'misadventure'. The doctor recommended constant protective armor, with no way in for little creatures. A bee keeper's outfit was the most cost-effective reliable solution. Unofficially, he suggested suicide by melting would be painless, as his nerve endings had gone, along with his skin, flesh and bones. But there was another way: he could go hard-boiled, but this carried a risk of paralysis. There were no precedents for this type of case, the doctor told him, a little too enthusiastically, like he was a subject wriggling through the magnifying glass.

In the end, it wasn't the bugs or the children that got him. Wacky Whalley had him trailed by agents in an ice cream van, so that when Dr B was alone, gently melting under his bee keeper's outfit on a hot summer's day in the park, they jumped out of their ice cream van and caught him.

Wacky Whalley's new limited edition Wacky Candy bar won the prestigious Interstellar award (sponsored by Galaxy, Mars, Milky Way and Starburst. Somehow, after the limited run of 2,000 bars they never quite found that special formula again, and their Wacky Candy Bars were never as popular again. Those who ate the limited edition bars were blissfully never made aware of the special ingredient.

-- Mark M. Lewis

Temporary Duty

Candy's touch on Mike's arm lingers too long as they sit side-by-side at the kitchen island popping *Peanut m&ms*, Candy's favorite. I'm uncomfortable, but I feel guilty. She and I are friends--friends since the 7th grade when we met in homeroom—7th grade, the year we learned how to use tampons—the year we saw that ninth grade boy French kissing Becky Rollands in the locker hall between classes and we laughed at all the spit on Becky's face. Candy doesn't mean anything by it when she whispers in Mike's ear while I stand over the stove making homemade spaghetti sauce for the three of us. She's in town on *Temporary Duty* from the Pentagon and will be gone tomorrow, so I selfishly sent the kids to the sitter's so we could catch up in peace without the kids using her as a jungle-gym all evening. "What's so funny?" I ask.

Leaning into him, showing her ample cleavage, "Nothing," is giggled in unison. I know I'm the butt of the joke.

Mike gets up from the island. I think he's going to grab a spoon, then me, and taste the sauce like he always does, but he strolls past me to the fridge, never making eye contact. "Want a beer?" He holds out a Pabst Blue Ribbon to Candy. She halts just enough for only me to notice, remembering it was Blue Ribbon bottles strewn in her yard like toddlers' toys when I'd drive over to get her to stay with me because her dad was drunk again, belligerent, and her mom was, well, who knows where.

My mom was happy to take her in, "Poor thing, she's no trouble," Mom would say. I never told Mom, or even Candy, that I knew she stole my favorite charm-bracelet and a few cheap barrettes one of those nights she stayed over. Funny, but I would have given them to her—given anything; she was my friend.

"No thanks, white wine, please, if you have any dry. Hey, is there a game on tonight?"

"Yep, Peyton's first game with the Broncos. Interested?" Mike replied.

They sit on the weathered, leather love-seat. Laps sharing *m&ms*, they touch from ankle to hip. But that's because the seat is so old and dips in the middle. I'm sure they don't realize they look like they're snuggling-up.

Candy sips her wine; Mike gulps his beer. Both cheering for Peyton. I set the table with the *Country Roses* china my mom left me. Candy may not be back in town for a while and I want things to be nice, nice memories, nice thoughts to replace the bad ones, or at least cloud them over.

"Time to eat, you two," I call.

"Be there in a minute," Mike calls. "We've got to watch the end of this drive." I'm jealous of the excitement in his voice. I'm rattled. The excitement is because of her, but she can't help that. She likes football, all sports, for that matter, always has. Maybe I should start watching the games with him from now on? Then, who knows, he might enjoy cooking with me. Perhaps we could go to cooking classes together? I pull out my chair. Sit. And wait on Peyton, Mike, and Candy.

After a fresh green salad drizzled with champagne dressing, warm, garlic-buttered Italian loaf, spaghetti with meatballs (I wonder if they noticed I peeled the Roma tomatoes and used fresh herbs from my garden), and a glass or two of Candy's gift of a fancy Cabernet Sauvignon that must have set her back a pretty-penny, we clear the table to relax with cream-cheese pound cake, Mike's great-aunt's recipe, and a cup of tea.

"Your mom's *Country Roses*. I remember," Candy says, lifting the gold rimmed cup to her lips, locking eyes with me just as she had the night she came home from college and I told her *I was so very sorry*. I had to tell her face to face. She had to hear it directly from me. *It just happened. I was marrying her boyfriend.* "Here, Mike," Candy encouraged, "taste my tea. It has honey in it. It's so much better for you than that processed, artificial sugar your wife gives you." She raises her cup, holds her other hand under his chin, letting him sip her honeyed tea.

-- Deborah R. Majors

Submerged

I don't want to lose face. Despite needles of fear. Sharp buzzing quiet. I tell myself it's okay—nervous because this is new, not dangerous. I know I'm lying. But he can't make me run. The pimples. His gym shorts. Junior high. He's way older than we are.

"Wanna have some?" he says. I'm afraid to look at his face, to see if he is talking to me. Probably not. Layla's prettier, she's *Little Miss Small County*. I was gonna enter. Mama took me to audition. Then she said it wasn't worth time and effort. Layla won. She was in the paper, tiara, fairy wand, pretty white dress.

"Huh?" Layla asked.

"Wanna have some?" In his hand. He doesn't look around. The street is silent. Layla tilts her head, eyebrow scrunched. "Some of this," he says, bouncing his hand. He loves her in a grown up way. She doesn't understand. She is a year younger than me.

It is long, straight. I've only seen small ones. He holds it like a treasure. Like a Holy Bible. This is wrong. We are alone. Just me and Layla. And this guy. Can't see him. Just what's in his hand, backed by black gym shorts.

I roll my eyes. A big, obvious, whole body I-don't-want-him-to-think-I-care-eye-roll. The kind my sister makes fun of. *Drama drama drama...*

I push my bike back up the long side of the ditch. Try to steady my hands. Pull my bike, myself into position, ready to launch down into the ditch and up the other side. Beside me I hear Layla say, "Wait, what?" Her voice is louder now. I swing around. He's riding away. Ten speed. Fast. Gone.

"What did he want to give us?" Layla asks. Pouty. Offered something then left. Rude.

"I think that's called flushing." My voice is shaking. It is a river, broken through the dam that divides our neighborhood from the next. "That was his thingy!"

"I thought it was a candy bar," she said. "I wanted to know what kind. I wanted a Snickers." Our favorite.

"We should tell," I say, already running to Layla's house, my bare feet slapping against the hot porch concrete. Barely inside, her mother shoos us out. She's already told us, she is working on homework with Layla's brother. Her southern accent is a hard frown of disappointment. Play outside. If she has to tell us again, we'll both be in for it. *Go!*

Outside. Hands shaking like hunger. I'm not hungry. I'm afraid. Of getting it. Of drowning. Of gym shorts.

"My house!" Can't stand still. Mama's not home. Daddy's in bath. Not supposed to bother him in the bath. I'm about to pee myself. Go to toilet. Nothing will come out. I will drown if I don't speak. Down the hall. Daddy's bathroom. Knock.

"A man showed us his thingy. He went away." Beneath shaking there is a lump, my second heart, pounding in my neck. Any bigger and I can't breathe. Slapping crash of quick movement in still tub water. From beneath the crack in the door a pool of water spreads. I have to pee. I can't.

Door to bathroom flies open. Bath water covers tile floor. Daddy runs, towel covering his parts. To front yard. Follow behind. Daddy yelling. Never seen him angry. Yelling at a ghost. Piercing the sharp quiet buzz. Sun is sinking. We are still here, standing in the messy place where boy in gym shorts stood.

Layla's mom and brother run toward us. *What is the yelling about?* Her eyes flash anger at me. *Why didn't you say so?* I can't speak. My words are under water.

55

Layla says, "You said don't bug you. We tried...." She trails off. No point, we are gonna get it now.

I want to explain, to catch my breath, for my words to match. I want to pee. Mostly right now I want to go inside. But I am afraid. *What did he look like? His face?* I only remember pimples and what he said. I only remember gym shorts. I will remember those forever.

*****

It becomes a joke when the neighborhood kids hear about Layla's candy bar confusion: *Skor Bar, King sized Chunky, Almond Joy, Mounds, Mr. Goodbar.* The trivialization will be a twisted form of comfort until I have a daughter, when I will inventory requests for candy based on experience, denying familiar names. Stocked shelves of chocolate bars become a reminder of what to do differently.

-- Jacqueline Markowski

Frying Pan Road

I caked it up,
ate to be filled —
stuffed in
my house
on Frying Pan Road.

There's meringue on
my cake, a julep in one
hand, a fork
in the other.

Light moves as
memory across the
early afternoon, alternating
between the past and a bowl
of shadows.

Jujubes pop
off a hot stove top
on Frying Pan Road.

I look at the clock
and wait with a glistening
brooch at my throat
for the other shoe
to slip across my painted
toenails and

drop.

-- Grace Maselli

We'd Love to Come but We Have Dietary Restrictions

We are happy, yes,
to tea and crumpet
at your house.
He can eat
eggs. I cannot. Not if
they are the main ingredient
in anything. I can eat gluten.
He cannot.

I am thrilled
with toast and butter. But I cannot
eat shellfish or berries. Blue and cran
are OK. But no eggplant
or tropical fruit. Pineapple
is OK.
And all melons.

I prefer to avoid
cucumbers
garlic
cilantro
cabbage
caffeine.

Sorry for the fuss!

Now what
can we bring?

Some herbal tea?
Waffles and
candies that
are gluten-free?

-- Grace Maselli

Shipwrecked

A Shipwreck Bag was a sack of supplies every Sunday -
bulls-eyes, sherbet, fake cigarettes and spicy licorice pipes,
pink or red beads on the bowl,
like my dad's pipe, which was filled and lit
and smoked and re-lit, smoked and emptied twenty times a day
to the sound of a rattling cough, copious spitting.

His thumb would be black,
his jacket pocket sometimes went on fire,
the Full Bent Cherry-Polished Pipe
left smoking away on its own.
We tapped and pulled and chewed on our pipes
and he tapped and pulled and chewed on his.

In his sixties he gave it up, buried the pipe
under a rose bush at the Blackrock Clinic,
then closed his eyes as they bypassed his heart.
He developed a sweet tooth like ours,
tasted a handful of years with his mended heart.
The cancer got his lungs then, too late for a Shipwreck Bag.

-- Shirley McClure

Working Like a Fool

Employment left a lousy taste
in my mouth, but money for food
& rent was a necessity, all I had
was a bar of chocolate & a wish

Writing sure hadn't put many
nickels in my pockets, I got out
the want ads & my magic rabbit's
paw, the hare had been unlucky

I'd herded skunks in Texas
for a French perfume company,
milked poisonous snakes for venom
antidotes, canned sardines in Maine

The paper had a hospital looking for
a drug tester, I thought what the hell,
I can do that, when I arrived a nurse
told me the job was for a piss taster

As hard up for money as I was, I had
to draw a line somewhere, later I
discovered someone had changed the
e to an a, on the application form.

                     -- Catfish McDaris

The Wrong Place

The lady on the corner
sucking on a lollipop
tried to walk across the
street in the crosswalks

The car didn't slow down,
even when she flew up into
the air & made a sick thud
splatter noise on the asphalt

I got most of the license
plate, I held her bloody head,
& removed her sucker &
prayed for help, I covered her
with my jacket while the police
& ambulance took forever

The police asked me, where
her purse was, I said I had no
idea, they took my statement

The lady was beyond help,
the cops followed the bloody
trail & found the drunken
woman driver asleep in her car

The hood was covered in
blood, hair, & brains,
the missing purse hung from
the right rear view mirror

I went from being a suspect,
to a hero, it didn't make much
difference to me or the two ladies.

-- *Catfish McDaris*

Ode to Chocolate

*for Pindar, Horace, Ben Jonson
Wordsworth, Keats, Shelley, and
especially Pablo Neruda*

O, chocolate, be not just
some complex, rich
concoction boasting high
infusions of that deep
dark pod, but something
more pedestrian, less odd,
petit bourgeois,
not that antique Nahuatl
seed Hernán Cortés thought
good as gold or better,
but milk chocolate or almost
impossibly white and never
semisweet or bitter, no,
nor bittersweet, not ever.

And lest we get too clever,
let it not be European,
Dutch or Swiss,
or even Caribbean.
Let us stick to common fudge,
or cake, or ordinary brownies,
American candy bars,
hot fudge sundaes, shakes,
or covered cherries,
peanut clusters,
cream-filled chocolates,
chocolate dreams
dipped in dim memories
of secular Easters
unfettered by the cross,
except in chocolate
wreathed in sugared lilies,

and Christmases
far away from the manger.

O, chocolate,
what would you be
without your secret recipes?
Thou art wicked at heart,
surely Satan's first fruit
squeezed from sugarcane and
meant to lead mankind astray,
first chocolate-covered apple,
aphrodisiacal,
pendent from the forbidden tree,
intended to pull humanity down,
we witless victims
brought low,
reduced to our elements,
these words, these sentiments,
this would-be delectable ode.

-- Ron McFarland

I (Still) Want Candy

It was, you know,
just another loud show,
but a woman with a Mohawk
had been watching from three rows in,
not just listening but burning a stare
with the intensity of a pitcher
ready to throw.

And when my drummer
hit the 3-on-2 Bo Diddley beat
usually borrowed for a Phish cover
she leapt on stage and stepped to the mike
like she belonged there, and it all flooded back –
the girl on the beach in the early 80's low-fi video,
she was only 16 then, there was never another hit, but
her chords and notes flew obediently from my fingers,
and from deep in her throat came the words,
the old familiar chorus that we all want
candy, and the audience sang along,
as if we'd rehearsed it, as if
not a day had gone by.

-- Matt McGee

The Traders

The type of people you find
in the grocery store's seasonal candy section
at 5:23 pm on Halloween night
resemble NYSE traders
in The Pit.

Pre-wrapped recognizable brand names,
perfect for month-long leftovers?
Buy! Buy! Buy!

Cheap-ass lollipops?
Sell! Sell!

With shelves nearing empty
and the witching hour approaching,
traders frenzy as if
a bread shortage is on
and winter fast approaching.

As they empty into the parking lot,
their trick-or-treat sacks
traded in for reusable grocery bags,
the leaves of another year
scrape underfoot,
speeding home
to another holiday
give-away.

-- Matt McGee

How Sweet!

After bathing in bubble gum,
Mary Jane unties ribbon candy
from bags of chocolate kisses.

Sky colored by yellow, pink
& blue cotton candy clouds.

Marshmallow chicks hide
behind spearmint leaves.

Jelly beans sprout along
fields of candy corn.

Caramel apples, lemon drops,
orange slices stacked for sale
at Lolly Pop's juicy fruit shop.

Watch out as sour gummy
worms wiggle underfoot.

Climbing big rock candy mountain
wandering with sugar high stars.

Thirsty now, Mary Jane sips
root beer barrels at Snickers Bar.

Black licorice fills this night
with confectionary dreams
& one big banana moon pie.

-- Joan McNerney

Gamed-Out

for Carol Cutts

Jill the Poet's forfeited her mojo recently,
gone totally gizmo playing Candy Crush Saga.

Sweet! Tasty!! Delicious!!! Divine!!!!
Seems the Widow Cutts turned Jillsy onto King's

crack game, sort of Candyland meets
Pac-Man meets Sudoku using shiny sugary jellies.

Sweet! Tasty!! Delicious!!! Divine!!!!

She's made it in a fortnight from Lemonade Lake
into the Chocolate Mountains to Level #45. What poetry!

Sweet! Tasty!! Delicious!!! Divine!!!!

-- Karla Linn Merrifield

You Burn Me

You burn me
You burn me

You burn me
with candle power and cinnamon

You burn me
with burnished kisses and dark chocolate

You burn me
with radiated wishes up in licorice smoke

You burn me
with cherry moonshining dreams and tomorrow

-- Karla Linn Merrifield

Childhood Chocolates

As I recall the Easter meal I ate was
chocolate, not cocoa chocolate but white chocolate,
safe chocolate, not really chocolate at all,
not like Mom's milk chocolate or Dad's dark-dark
chocolate, that chocolate of allergy attacks,
call-the-ambulance chocolate, Benadryl chocolate,
oxygen-tent chocolate, no not my brother's Brach's,
Whitman's, Stover's, Mars' and Hersheys' chocolate.

A solid white chocolate, twelve-inch bunny keeps
up to six months in the Frigidaire. I made it last—
long after the chocolate-chocolate morsels melted
in my brother's mouth on that singular day when
he began to hate me.

-- Karla Linn Merrifield

Three Poets

I used to eat while reading. Once, a flake of chocolate
fell off and smudged a page. Yes, I was an idiot.
Reflecting, though, I started thinking, How appropriate
The Wasteland should be smudged by sweetness, soiled for all its wit.

Once, reading Emily outside and bothered by a bee,
I swore that it was trying to read too—aloud—to me.
And one time Dorothy made me laugh so hard I had to shut
the book, upon which I received the nastiest paper cut.

My Dickinson's still white of course—and black. My Eliot
as well, with here and there an extra black or dark-brown blot.
My Parker's also white and black, but marked in streaks of red
which, every time I open her, appear to pulse and spread
as if to scream how wrong I'd been, leaving her for dead.

-- James B. Nicola

Just One Chocolate, Slowly

Lips parted –
to be painted with melted luxury.
Eyes wide to the curve and gloss –
the sheen of velvet brown truffle.

Teeth –
gentle at first touch –
release liquid caramel.
The tongue welcomes a rich river of gold.

The mind knows
this single, round gift –
sun spun into sugar,
love caressed and curled around
a dark, dense center,
the afterglow of chocolate
pointing starward.

-- Cristina M.R. Norcross

Death by Turtle

Here, just bury this,
I say.

A plastic wrapped package
with gold letters
contains a milk chocolate-caramel-peanut confection,
also known as widening-of-waist
or –
death by chocolate turtle.

The purple and gold box
sits innocently on the counter.
Calorific enticement stares at me –
a sexy, small box
covered with fancy food photography.

Hiding it on the bottom pantry shelf,
next to the fire extinguisher,
doesn't help one bit.
I know where the turtle lives.
Not the basement either –
there are stairs to navigate,
but I could always waltz down
during a commercial break
and open the cabinet above the bar.

Drastic measures ensue.
Scotch tape,
then wide, packing tape adorn the box,
followed by the dark, plastic stretch of a Hefty bag.
Leave no trace.

Holding my breath, I peak outside the window
where my husband's jacket fades
into the treacherous woods behind our pond.

It's done, he says.
Let's speak no more of it.

There is always the leftover stash
from Halloween.

-- Cristina M.R. Norcross

Cookies for Breakfast

They are serving cookies for breakfast
here at the poetry festival,
cookies and brownies and cakes
they call muffins, the size of D-cups.
Vanilla or hazelnut syrup
are available to flavor the coffee.
Life is good, life is rich, it all suggests—
enjoy it to the fullest! And I want to.
I really do.

I hate to sound like an old naysayer,
scorning the sweetness of life,
restricting breakfast to oatmeal
with a few dried cranberries
or six measured ounces
of Light and Fit yogurt,
muttering to myself, "What next,
turkey stuffed with M & Ms
for Thanksgiving dinner?"

Please—let me not miss
a moment of the celebration.
But I don't want cookies for breakfast.

-- George H. Northrup

First Kiss

I gave her a kiss on
Valentine's Day
that honey-lipped lass
of my just
stirring dreams.

Wordless,
heart weighted,
barely not shaking.
Brazen,
emboldened,
yet painfully shy.

But unlike most girls
who would save such a trinket
a foil-covered taste
to remember me by

she ate it.

-- Vincent O'Connor

Too Sweet

I should've walked away. I know that now. Not for the likes of me, not that one.

It's dark by the river. Clumped trees and a line of boxy caravans shred the blare of the fairground to a ghost hum. I roll my shoulders and stretch out my back, I'll have to soak for a week. Never expected the bitch to be that heavy.

Candy pressed up close when I took her fare on the carousel: pink lips, soft breath, warm tongue. Intoxicated, full of the taste of her, I did what she wanted. All of it. Can't judge a book by its cover, that's what Ma always used to say. Now there was a bitter old hag. She was right though—look what I found under the cellophane wrap of glitter and deceit.

Honeyed kiss acid on my tongue, coating my teeth, making them ache.

I can't wake up, not properly, no matter how hard I scrub at my face. Candy laughs, sugar in my ear. Can't go, not yet. She has more scores to settle. Another kiss, another rush. I'm buzzing. Candy-pink fingernails point out another girl in the fairground crowd.

Too late to walk away.

Slices of midnight between familiar silent caravans. As good a place as any. A punch to the stomach to keep her quiet. Pull the knife. One, two and it's done. Don't know what the girl did to deserve this. Don't care.

Sugar bitter at the back of my throat. Decide that it's death that adds the extra pounds, a final 'up yours' to the one who cut her life short. A soft splash and she's swallowed by the cess-pit of a river.

Candy is waiting, skin flash painted red and gold in the lights of the Ferris wheel. She holds me while I cough and spit, blood and black cracked teeth splatter the flattened grass. And I think: Time to walk away.

She plants her lips on mine.

'One more,' she whispers. 'One more.'

Sugar swamped and grinning, I follow her back to the thinning crowd. What else can I do? She's too sweet for me, and no mistake.

-- Susan Oke

Easter Egg Hunt

finds marshmallow chicks
jelly beans candy eggs
fills his basket stuffs his
mouth suddenly spews
blue shell yellow yolk
from a fallen robin nest
under the old elm tree

> *-- Carl Palmer*

Mischief Moments

Candice ogled the box resting next to the handsome young man sitting opposite her. The light radiating from the oval shape promised paradise on earth.

This box was special, for it was a limited edition which had been withdrawn within weeks of its launch, making it very rare indeed. 'Mischief Moments' had acquired notoriety following the sudden disappearance of its creator.

The Web had buzzed and sizzled with conspiracy theories. Some claimed the new flavours of chocolate defied description, yet were so scrumptious that fearful competitors had taken unspeakable steps. Others claimed the Consumption Intelligence Agency (CIA) had closed down the manufacturer following reports of unusual side effects.

"Hey, you've left this behind!" Candice called, chasing after the young man.

"What are you talking about?" His piercing blue eyes searched hers to the depths of her soul, whilst an enigmatic smile played across his lips.

Up close he smelt of vanilla with a hint of caramel, her favourite scent in the whole world. She'd assumed it was a gift for his girlfriend but his denial was emphatic as he quickly walked away.

Candice looked around but she was alone. An eerie silence at odds with the joyous sunshine sent a chill down her back. Mesmerised by the velvety softness of the wrapping, Candice caressed the red ribbon bow. Unwittingly, she loosened it. With a loud pop the lid flew open. An unbelievable aroma set her head spinning. She watched helplessly as tinsel covered globes cascaded out and rolled out of sight. All, except one had escaped.

This solitary piece vibrated, tickling her big toe. Candice nervously nudged the golden globe away but it boomeranged back and upwards, bounced off the tip of her nose and landed in the palm of her hand.

"Now you've done it," a whining screech proclaimed the beginning of a nightmare, for this solo globe spoke, and not too politely at that.

"You've set those chocolates free. They create mayhem with their unpredictable behaviour."

"It's not my fault," Candice protested, running her tongue over her lower lip for she could taste the scent of strawberries covered in white chocolate. Unable to resist she sank her teeth into the talking globe.

There goes my diet! Her thoughts whispered as droplets of heaven melted in her mouth. Clouds of candyfloss sweetness engulfed her. Through the pink mist Candice glimpsed the young man.

"This way, before they see us," he cried, dragging Candice behind a high sided vehicle just as a black van rolled by.

"Who are you? What's going on?" demanded Candice.

"I am the creator of Mischief Moments and I am being chased by CIA for my recipe."

"What's so special about the recipe?"

"The ingredients can be programmed at the nano particle level and have the potential to be weapons of mass devastation. I installed self programming, self perpetuating code to prevent Governments from exploiting this capability. Unfortunately, a degree of random wilfulness and unforeseen capabilities has been generated."

"So why did you deny the box was yours?"

"Because I thought you were one of them."

A loud rumbling cut short their conversation as the van, having turned back, headed towards them. Candice and the young man cowered in their hideout as the dark mass approached menacingly.

"Hey! You there. Over here," a treacherous voice called out from Candice's mouth as the golden globe, having reformed, zigged and zagged across her tongue. Candice tried to gulp the globe back down but instead she gagged and the globe came spurting out. Rolling over to the van with the rapidity of a Cheetah, the globe came to a sudden halt and waited patiently. The heavily armoured occupants poured out and readied their weapons.

"Where are those renegade chocolates?" the leader demanded.

Gripping fear froze Candice.

Undecipherable cries surrounded the group as the escapee globes suddenly appeared from all directions. Then, uniting in rebellion, they surged and whirled, whipping up a deliciously scented pink mist. Angry and scared screams filled the air as opposing forces battled for dominance.

Candice and the young man watched motionless as the hubbub finally subsided and the pink mist cleared to reveal a field of sleeping security men.

"You see not all their actions are mischievous," the golden globe called out to Candice, as he led his motley collection of chocolates back into the oval box.

Candice and the young man exchanged unspoken words, snapped shut the lid on 'Mischief Moments' and hurried away from the cacophony of snores.

-- Mangal Patel

Cocoa Shadows and Chocolate Cosmos

The ground was cocoa shadows
and savory browns—
laced with bold limes, frail creams, warmest licorice.

Above, an airship,
absorbing greyest clouds of steam,
melting a chocolate cosmos
onto strawberry-flavored smiles.

-- Richard King Perkins II

Lines of Lost Chocolate

Me and Freddie find a huge bar
of baker's chocolate melting near
the corner of Parkside and Augusta.
We're six years old
and at least know we can't eat it
so instead we plaster each other
in warm chocolate for an hour or more.
When our moms' see us
they hose us down in the yard,
pissed that their eldest children
could do anything as stupid as this.
More than forty years later,
it has become one of the stories
that helps recall the person
that I no longer am.

—Still, occasionally,
I catch myself scanning hot pavement,
hoping to find someone's
lost bar of melting chocolate
and for my wife to finger wag at me
as to what in the world I was thinking
as the Hershey's begins to cast itself
in multiple striations
across her clothing and skin.

-- Richard King Perkins II

Candy-Gram on Wheels

Aboveground taste testing, nukable zoom
chocolate delivered on antique motorcycle
sidecars customized into neon candy shacks
with engines hot as oven delight offering up
highly affordable excess unwrapped, sizzling,
celebrating gourmet desserts: never gluttony
unless honey glazed, licking the biggest spoon
fantastic smoothly through all the hard times

-- David S. Pointer

Leaf Licker

James licks the lettuce leaf, lays it flat upon his plate. He likes the texture, not the taste. He likes living in the now.

Sarah glares pointedly across the cafeteria table. "You think you're cool? Is that it?" All along the opposing lines, peers watch with raised forks, spoons, an occasional butter knife. Girls on one side, boys the other. She stands, and the sound of chair legs sliding sends a shriek through the hall. Faces turn from other tables, from people walking with their trays.

"Well, you're not cool, James Dearborn, this is cool." She rips her blouse up to expose a thumb-sized jade inset into her belly button.

"Wow," someone whispers. "A little higher," a boy says.

Sarah turns her glare onto him. She lifts her blouse until the bottom edge of a bra cup shows. "Is that what you want, you little perv?"

"Almost," the boy says. His cheeks are as red as the ketchup on his plate.

"Show me yours," Sarah says, "I'll show you mine." She winks to her girl friends. "I'm sure this side of the table could use a laugh."

The boy shrivels into himself. Shoulders hunched, face slanted down, he lifts a fish sandwich to his lips.

"And you," Sarah says, returning to James. "What's the f-ing deal with you, huh?" She lets her blouse slide down. "You have a condition we should know about or something? You act like that lettuce is a piece of candy."

James gives her a half smile. "I could show you," he says. His voice is quiet enough that it would never have been heard a few minutes before. He turns the lettuce leaf in his hands. Sarah's hands cup her belly, an absent gesture that James does not miss. Someone coughs a mile away. "Show me what?" she says.

James licks, tongue moving slow across the green. "How," he says, and his eyes find Sarah as if they have never found anyone before.

-- Stephen V. Ramey

Our Mounds Candy Bar

Once upon a time, before learning about
the dangers of sugar, before counting calories,
I reveled in Mounds candy bars,
the package containing always two mounds:
stripping the chocolate carefully
with my teeth, gradually moving to
the coconut interior, the heart of the bar,
the way a million children have eaten
those little hills of candy.

Unlike other candy bars of my childhood,
these had their special setting, emerging from
my father's overalls pocket on the cow path
as we herded our two dozen Holsteins,
meandering, sluggishly shuffling
their way to the barn for evening milking.

Dad would pull out a Mounds, tear open
the package, hand me one of the pieces.
He would eat his like an adult,
biting right into it, no layering, one,
two, maybe three bites and it was gone.
The chocolate would often be melted
against the wrapper, but the taste lost nothing
in the journey, and the coconut as sweet
as ever. Even today, decades later, I cannot see
a Mounds at a check-out counter without longing
for one more trip up a cow path.

-- Edward J. Rielly

Sweet Tooth

I just know you
won't be denied
any candy, won't deprive yourself
of any pleasure so specific
it has its own little dukedom
on your tongue.

Those chocolate turtles you love, for instance,
with their pecan shells
fastened by caramel
on a body of deep cacao

or the Australian licorice
so obsidian dark it's almost the
opposite of sweet.

You collect tiny boxes
of almond nougat
with paintings on the covers
of Spanish barons.

Or are your favorites the Frangos,
with their tropical chocolate
coating the peppermint from the chill north,
a box you buy changing planes in Chicago.

But you always stop near our house
at the old ravioli factory
for those imported Italian bonbons
delicious as their flavor names:
limone, pera, fragola, albicocca.

You say you've never tasted candy again
quite the way you did as a child,
when your mother brought your favorite treats

in clear wrappers twisted at both ends,
those firecrackers of flavor.

-- Zack Rogow

Narrow Escape from a Near Miss

She wasn't a very good shot.
Thank goodness it entered and left quickly,
like minimally invasive surgery.
The trick is to stay perpendicular
with your upper body
and to live across the street
from a fortune cookie factory.
It's odd how I felt so symphonic,
as if I were a red toolbox
lost in a cold, metallic sleep.
My thoughts became diagrams.
I was a photograph of a cease-fire,
violated.
Now, what's left of me
feels like waiting-room time,
a dimmer-switch in a funeral home.

Who's to say? Was it cabin fever,
or a girlfriend crime-wave?
I'll never know.
She's the cutest darn thing, too,
like illegal fireworks
detonating in a crowded candy store.
She's the side of town
everybody tells you to stay away from,
a theater on fire, audience trapped inside.
I tell myself, *At-ease, soldier.*
It may look like a murder,
but it's probably just buyer's remorse.

-- Brad Rose

Old Dirk Savors the Prospect of Honeymoon Bliss with His Second Teen Bride.

Candy cigarette trembling in her haunted hand,
adorable secrets loosely locked
in that smiling sin vault,
her giddy little-girl laugh track loops,
like a busy signal when you phone
the emergency room.

She's mine now, all mine.

Sweet ghost lounging
beneath the cool avalanche of starched sheets,
she's naked as a cupcake on death's island.
This isn't the first time
I've shopped for tombstones
at Toys R Us.

-- Brad Rose

Pink Candy Hearts

It's just a matter of time
before it's a big legal mess.
I think I know what's happening,
but I don't.
She says, "Sweetheart, you know better
than to try to change the weather in a doll house."
Her skinny scalpel of a smile,
slicing through my life's gray, imperfect fog,
before the lawyers move in,
eat all the little candy hearts.
Some of them, you'd swear, almost beating.

-- Brad Rose

It's for Me, Cupid

Just outside the Disneyland candy store, the pretty young woman gently licks the recently purchased, red, heart-shaped lollipop. She licks it like a cat licking its paw. I watch her, and dream of paws. I yearn to be a paw. The summer breeze tosses her hair. The white straps of her summer sundress slouch from her impossibly delicate shoulders. As she notices my leer, her darting smile becomes an arrow. A serrated arrow. It pierces my heart.

My wife phones.

-- Brad Rose

Campbell River

Across Vancouver Island on Campbell River
lumberjacks jump from log to log
strong bodies, sharp poles
propelled rafts of fresh cut trees
down the river, over white rapids
sparkling drops of river water
suspended in the air.

I was five, watching the world rush by
collecting stones from the smooth banks.
I knew some good spots for pretending.

Lumberjacks danced on Campbell River
chips of wet wood flew
iron cleats, polished silver
glistened in the rays of sun.

We sat on the banks
three young friends tow-headed
tanned from days outside
gazing from the mouth of Campbell River
to the blue Pacific
lost in our dreams
pop bottles lay in the river ditches
turned in at the corner store
we savored red licorice and penny candy.

My mother's voice echoing across the trees
called me home
a couple nickels in my pocket
brown arms, thin legs
smeared with river silt
the neighbor's yellow lab at my heels
behind me the screen door slammed
dinner on the table

today lumberjacks had danced
on Campbell River.

> *-- Janice D. Rubin*

Sweet Sting

Ms Candice is at the front of the class testing us on mathematical facts but I know it all already and I'm whispering to Alice in the back row.

"How long do you think we've been in this school? How much longer do you think we'll have to stay here?"

She's looking puzzled and I wonder whether I should confide or not. "This is where we live, Joel," she responds. "One day we'll be grown up and maybe we'll be teachers like Ms Candice."

As if alerted by the speaking of her name, our icy mistress shoots a sharp look our way. She taps her straight, striped cane against the board to demand attention. I've had my run-ins with her lately. She caught me sleepwalking a couple of times. I didn't reveal what I saw. But I'm about to tell Alice .

"I don't think we're ever going to be allowed to leave," I hiss. "I've seen things."

"You've dreamed things."

She's wearing a short-sleeved top that shows off the area on her left arm where the medics regularly take "samples" to ensure our continuing health. Her skirt is short and although her knees are bony and girlish I find that I am beginning to notice the smoothness of her legs. It's a factor I'd never considered before. Maybe I am changing. Last night I dreamt that I saw Ms Candice unclothed –

"Joel!" the teacher calls. "Come on, it's your celebration day. Come and break the piñata."

How can it be my day again? So little time has passed. But then it's always someone's special day, on some sort of rotation.

I walk to the front of the room, aware of the young eyes fixed upon me. Precious children we are, that's why they keep checking our health by taking skin scrapings. Except on my wanderings I found places that confused me. Children who looked like me and my friends but how could that be? Children in tanks, floating, not exactly alive and not exactly formed –

"Joel, snap out of it," Ms Candice orders. "Take the stick."

I swing and smash the container within one mighty blow. My classmates yell gleefully and rush to gather the sweets from where they have fallen. There are plenty to go round for everyone. Alice grabs a handful. Ms Candice refrains; and so do I.

"Take a sweetie, Joel, they're for everyone."

Her voice is like a soft brush, a warm bath, chocolate on the tongue or teeth. I pick up one of the wrapped candies, close it in my fist, make to swallow it but discard it softly when the teacher's eyes are turned away. This is what I wanted to tell Alice : that the sweets are the instruments of their control. And doubtless other foods. Keeping us sweet... young... helpless.

"Class dismissed! And don't ruin your teeth on those candies."

I make to follow my excited yet passive fellows.

"Joel? A moment, please."

She stands at full height and I feel something stirring in me that I've only lately become aware of. Ms Candice is gorgeous. Not because she is a fully-grown, perfect adult but because she is a woman and is beginning to show me attention... attention that I am starting to crave. She is my beautiful enemy.

"You know the rules, Joel," she breathes. "No wandering of voice or mind during lessons."

"What about hands?" I ask.

She flicks long black hair away from shadowy eyes. "Oh, I can see you are going to need my special treatment."

"Really?"

I don't want this but somewhere deep down, suppressed, I know that in fact I actually do.

"Bend over," she orders and the little boy that I still am complies.

She raises her striped candy cane; swishes it. One hit, two, three. The stick shatters and she twists the broken shards so that they penetrate my compliant skin. Bliss. Pain that is pleasure. Sweet bliss. Making me forgetful...

"Thank you, Ms," I answer.

"It's all for your own good, Joel. Now run along and be a good boy. And if you are there might be some special sweeties for you later."

-- Len Saculla

The Last Days

In my last days, my head
in the lap of solitude,
how was I to know cancer
would grow? You pour the
good years back into me:
the taffy we shared at
the beach, the fables you'd
tell, the red licorice we'd
put to each other's lips,
our taste for tomorrow.
Now the world passes
away from my eyes and
visitors leave glittering
flowers by my hospital
bed, and dainty white
truffles I've no appetite
to eat. Certain words
disappear when I can no
longer keep my passions
alive. Morning comes
and my nurse wheels me
to my mirror, a half dead
me. I wait for the unseen
heaven, wishing that
nothing had changed.
Infant stars melt away,
and, when I sleep, I dream
of repast, a fudge divinity
served on a glass saucer
before I am gone.

-- Bobbi Sinha-Morey

Missing

Five days after he disappeared
a Pez dispenser still lay on his
bed, nuggets of candy still left
inside. What good is a desperate
heart when two weeks have
gone by? No sign of my eleven-
year-old son, and every day I
search for him underneath
the uncaring sky. Hours before
sunrise I press my tears with
my fists; his favorite candy,
a box of Junior Minds, near his
picture right by my bedside
where I can see it. On a cold
night I write down a prayer,
weigh it down with a chocolate
Easter egg he once stole.
How difficult parting is as
weeks turn into months
without any hope.

-- Bobbi Sinha-Morey

Candied Snippets of Nature . . .

(i)

caramel covenants
of chameleon clouds echo
as honeydew kisses of raindrops,
on monsoon-parched earth.

(ii)

azure of sugar-lorn sky sucks
a orange candy sun,
that melts away to moods
of whimsical hourglass,
as tangerine tinted tongue
reveals its sweet-tooth at twilight.

(iii)

like marbles of mischief
within hip pockets
of harlequin night-sky,
the planets and astral bodies
are lozenges tinting lives
in varied flavors.

(iv)

chocolate éclairs
with saccharine softness within
are reminiscent of
ripeness of hard nuts to crack
like introverted coconuts
and passion fruit secrets.

(v)

winter mornings
blushing in subtle cerise
of juvenile cheeks,
with a lingering crisp freshness,
taste of peppermint kisses
stolen at duvet-clad dawn.

(vi)

sugarcoated raisins,
marshmallows, cherries,
strawberries and more
are molted memories of winters,
preserved on souvenir shelves
to season insipidities
of sweaty summer days.

-- Smita Sriwastav

Candy Foil Memories . . .

Memories wrapped in old candy foil,
pasted within pages
yellowed, dogeared and moth-eaten,
are like whispers echoing
from alleys of forgotten minutes,

the lines long scribbled
beneath glued chocolate paper
have a remembrance to revive,
an amnesic story to retell,

they walk me through
long deserted gravel trails
of an adolescence lost
with its giggly reverberations.

wizened fingers caress them
I can taste their long lost sweetness again
while a wistful smile glows
with precious moments relived.

a childish bet won, a silly prank played,
a gift of friendship or a favor repaid,
people forgotten, lost or gone,
faces misted by myopia of preoccupations~

fleet in snippets of recollections
like an old mute movie or a stilted song
from arthritic gramophone,
as I indulge in kaleidoscopic delights
of varied fragments of reverie...

-- Smita Sriwastav

The Kick of Éclairs

Sailing within realms
of amniotic complacence
while anxieties soared outside
like moods of barometric mercury,
you were seemingly
too lazy to bother with
a breast or butterfly stroke
inside aureate fluidities,
while I eagerly awaited
that softly knocked greeting
which strummed a caramel rain-song
on frowning lips of worry.

Palms cold and clammy,
sought to feel the faintest of moves
tracing enceinte contours,
as murmured prayer was
whispered in ears of taut silence,
brine filled eyes
refused to shed tears lest they
be a harbinger of ill omen,
the clocks tick tattooed drum beats
as apprehension mounted
and anxious limbs sped towards
alleys of recourse or remedy.

The echo of heart beat
was placating and musical sounding
through maze of inanimate wires,
as a hesitant smile dawned
reminiscent of crescent moon
on tempestuous night-skies,
reassuring, professional words revealed
your innocent mischief
and with no bitter pills to swallow
sucking a proffered éclairs

and pockets full of chocolate I returned
with you now apparently
riding an imagined bicycle inside
revitalized to spurn lethargy
after the sumptuous kick of candy.

-- Smita Sriwastav

My Mother Told Stories

Our mother remembered cars with no radios,
so she told stories.
We munched on her favorite candy,
Necco wafers, the color
and flavor of spring-coat buttons,
muted pastels, pink gray white green.

She told stories
all the way past
the road to Whalom Park.
Its wooden roller coaster
(she said)
had killed a soldier
just home from the war.

She told stories
as we crossed over
the Nashua River
that ran red
or blue or green
depending on the paper
Wallace's mill was making.
(As a girl in a pinafore,
my grandmother had waded in that water.)

Mother told stories
as she drove
past the site of Mal's Goody-Goody
where she used to play under the tables
while the adults played bridge
and slipped the children
pennies and Necco wafers
to match their Sunday best
muted pastels plaids and checks.

Our mother told stories
all the way to Grandmother's house.
We sat in the front seat,
crunching the last of the wafers,
discs less sweet
than our breakfast cereal.
We hoped for more
but sometimes tasted
the pale licorice, pale lavender
that Mother recalled.

-- Marianne Szlyk

On Gray Thursdays

Chinatown lights glow
like hard candies
red green purple yellow white
against the meringue of fog.

The colors sting
in February, not quite March,
when the last ice and snow
and wrappers crunch
like the sugar coating
on a cheap spice drop.

The colors coat the tongue
in sweater-weather May,
almost June,
when humid air congeals
like the bubble tea
that hides between cubes
of not-yet melted ice.

This is not the place
for October coffee
or December chocolate,
Mozart marizpan
or trail mix with quinoa
and chili flakes.

This is the place
to carry too much
and walk too quickly,
wearing black
wearing platform wedges
withdrawing from sugar

through all the gray Thursdays
no matter the season.

-- Marianne Szlyk

The Poet Dances with Inanimate Object

The poet dances with inanimate object,
iron poised over the navy blue skirt
with its stubborn wrinkles.
Hope triumphs over experience
once again.

The ironing board wobbles.
Sometimes it sticks,
victim of too many moves back and forth,
East and West, North and South,
always back to the same city.

Sunday night in the neighborhood,
not quite the same old apartment,
she remembers the used record stores
that now sell bacon chocolates
and lavender and sea salt caramels.
There she browsed for LPs,
mostly ones he owned in high school,
now over forty years ago,
sometimes ones she'd dance to
alone, without him.

She remembers taking the bus
with him to do laundry.
She remembers bringing along
a bag of half-price Easter eggs
from Moynihan's Drugs
for the long, May afternoon.

Their sweetness cloyed.
They left the (mostly) full bag
beside the brittle science fiction
paperbacks they read while waiting.
She wonders if she could find him
waiting at the Laundromat

or browsing the books and LPs
that crowd the last thrift store
standing on the avenue.

Hope triumphs over experience
once again.

-- Marianne Szlyk

Diabetic's Fantasia

In dream was candy sanctioned, encouraged even. Candy of all sorts.
For the chocolate lovers, there were pralines, nougats, truffles, and
bonbons. For others, there were brittles, caramels, licorice,
jelly beans, mints, rock candy, sourballs, taffies, and toffees.
All this, to name but a few.
The sheer variety was on an unprecedented scale, far beyond the halls
of candy we had experienced on trips to the Continent or the teeming
confectionaries off the alleys in regions yet further afield.

Youth, whose whiteness of teeth was rivaled by the whiteness of their lab
coats, proffered these delicacies with smiling indifference. There were no
inquiries into our medical history, no question of whether we had funds or
insurance. We were here to partake. This was the proverbial candy store
of our childhood; only we now had the discernment to truly savor
its nuances. We reached out to accept with a newfound abandon,
dispelling the anxiety that had come to recently to define us.
Finger-pricking instruments were on hand. Just in case.

The tastes were of course also unprecedented. We could
detect layers of flavor; an intricacy of the highest order. We could
isolate strands of hazelnut prancing through truffle, mint veins
extended through chocolate rendered buoyant by the freshest milk.
We could trace the interconnectedness of each element,
the lacework of it all. And we did see them as elements, not merely
ingredients. Perhaps we would need lab coats of our own?
Our exclamations murmured through the echoing marble aisles.

We were the opposite of Lucy and Ethel in the chocolate factory. There was
no impulse towards binging, no fear of being caught, for as was suggested
earlier, there was no question of wrongdoing. Far from it. Our doctors, at
the marble-topped tables, smiled at us in approval. Or at least that was
how we interpreted their smiles. Still, we noticed that they were merely
onlookers. We wondered what they were writing in their notebooks. We
noted suddenly the absence of cakes and cookies. Our calm began to
dissipate. Slowly, we drifted from delirium; slowly, we groped for insulin.

-- *Yermiyahu Ahron Taub*

Candy Tattoo

Never get into a car with strangers.
Beware of the temptations they may offer,
Mother warned, then burning to her theme:
they may beckon with treats, ones you know to be sanctioned,
such as those from Paskesz or Goldenberg's dark chocolate peanut chews.
They may even appear to be members of our community,
alluring in modest garb. They may even call you by your name,
but if you don't know who they are, do not get into the car.
Do you understand? Show me you understand. Good. Still not entirely
satisfied, Mother would return, trembling, to the concoction of the dish
at hand. For now, let us say barley soup or brisket or …

Would that I had listened to those Mother words.
Of the many proscriptions to which we were tethered, this one evoked not
merely sin or stain but danger. We who were showered with eggs and
tomatoes from university dorm rooms, we who were hounded en route
to school (even when we thought we knew which streets to bypass),
we who knew to travel in packs, we were no strangers to danger.
Yet this was different. Perhaps it was the pairing of strangers with candy,
the notes of terror flecked throughout the sweet familiar.
Perhaps it was the entering into car, the being whisked into gone-ness.
There was no proliferation of photos on kosher milk cartons back then.
But somehow we knew.

Would that I had listened to those Mother words.
There were other rooms I might have entered on that brink-of-autumn
night, a room such as a café on the avenue, redolent with bean,
purring with machine and the strumming of guitar. Or a back room,
darkened perhaps, but governed by restraint. But alas such rooms
were not selected that night. Instead after disembarking a crosstown bus,
another room, tucked between warehouses, proved irresistible. Here,
TV screens flickered above ballads of lost love lament drifted through
Marlboro mist men slouched in corners with booze and or smoke in
hand observing assessing nodding turning away gazing then staring
returning until finally he approached a mask of scruff and blur

his torch alighted upon me could it be yes he was upon me and was now whispering candy words nuzzling them into my neck etching them into skin where they emblazoned their intention with a singularity of purpose so that the ballads the smoke the touch which should have been enough for now for this first encounter only they weren't and so I devoured the candy a glutton became I mistaking sugar for care following outdoors his broad back t-shirt loose over his belt the clomp of feet on pavement into the car gleaming inscrutable so that those Mother words were not forgotten or discarded even but overruled so that I glimpsed Mother in glint after the lighting of Sabbath candles in anticipation of rest as the youngest born to her near middle age glided into catastrophe

-- Yermiyahu Ahron Taub

I Want Candy

Candy is dressed all in pink – pink stockings rising to meet the thigh hugging hem of her tight pink dress, vanilla hair puffed and billowing like a cotton cloud, frosted crystals of cheap pick and mix jewellery resting on the plump cleavage of her marshmallow breasts.

There's a vicious little splinter in the hard stick that holds her head high. It will pierce the greedy tongue of anyone who tries to take too much of her in one go. Beneath the orange soda glow of the street lamp she paces in ever-decreasing candy cane spirals, teetering on the caramel constructs of stiletto heels and wafting the irresistible entice of her sickly sweet scent to the night.

A man appears, wide-eyed and drooling, trembling with unfettered desire.

"You look scrumptious," he gasps. "How much to taste your sweetness?"

Candy smiles.

The white peppermint lozenges of her teeth reveal themselves between the cherry-red glossiness of her lips. She whispers a sum and flutters eyelids painted a bubblegum hue. With a jangle from her bangles the syrupy stickiness of her hand melds with the clammy sweat on his palm.

She leads him deep into the liquorice black of the alley.

His will dissolves and liquefies like chocolate become velvet in the intense heat of her embrace. The jellybean lacquer of her fingernails drives into his flesh. She allows him to unwrap her and claim the sticky prizes within.

He simmers a while before she brings him to the boil. She departs the moment he is spent and leaves him a single grain of her sugar. It wedges itself in the cavity of his cold and emotionless heart. In time the lustful cravings that it arouses will bring him back again and again and again.

"You're so sweet," he will whisper. "So, so sweet."

He is not the first and he won't be the last.

Each time he indulges she will leave him with the gift of another granule that will hasten the rot that decays his soul. He will age at alarming rate, becoming wan and haggard and frail. The delicious delight that his torture brings her will help Candy maintain the glow of her sugary sheen. It's all part of the bargain. Enter the candy shop and pay the price.

He will come to view what is left of his life through the peanut brittle fug of some diabolically diabetic coma and will find himself at death's doorstep much sooner than he ever expected. In his final moment the words that ooze like molasses in the last exhalation of his death gasp will be tragic in their inevitability.

"I want Candy."

And she will mourn him in pink - dusting her face in sherbet powders - rouging her cheeks in lollipop red.

-- David Turnbull

A Tourist in India

Women in saris are like pastel eggs, pulses
of color through the market, carrying family
on their minds, on their hips, gold
on wrists and necks, hands wrapped
and wrapped in tendrils of henna
as delicate and sheer as lace. The Taj Mahal
looks like Candy Land, marshmallow columns
and minarets of meringue. In the distance,
the graham cracker slums are built to crumble
in the mouth. Yes, I could eat this city.

Forgive me when I fall asleep drinking gin
in Mumbai, and wake up transformed
into a juniper tree. I don't know how to eat
with Kohl rimmed eyes, to see with bangled
hands, to accept my smallness
in this life and musical din. Forgive me,
I can only love what I believe I can eat.

-- Annaliese Wagner

Lunch with My Mother and Her Friends

Joe a Russian Jew
and German Joe
sit together every day

soldiers from opposing armies
in the same war
the same city

they may have even
fired at each other
half a world away

wheelchairs side by side
they have Kiev between them now
in common

I break them squares of chocolate.
Maybe they think
I'm their daughter.

Anna likes sweets. She used to dance
and still assumes
different shapes;

no longer defying gravity
she flops in a padded chair
with wheels

stretches
for the feeding spout
blindly, like a fledgling.

When Swan Lake played in
Olympic ice-skating on TV
she cried.

The little lady with no legs
at the next table
likes chocolate too.

I spoon food into my mother
from five scoops of
pureed colours like a palette

white whip of uber-mashed potatoes
peas or beans, something green
anyway, also orange

perhaps carrots or
a form of squash, with
mysterious beige meat

topped by a joyous
squiggle of gravy like the sign
on peppermint chocolate.

I'm the only person
at the table
with teeth.

-- Mercedes Webb-Pullman

Choosing Memories Like Chocolates

soft or hard centre
which day do you want?
picnic at Thredbo Diggings?
crocheted bikinis, long tall glasses
of rose and cider, mixed

you wore a black wig, we
dropped acid, studied ants
with a dog named Harold Wilson

three people in deep sleep therapy
died at Chelmsford House that day

ski seasons pass like dreams
high on altitude
there's always powder
on the next mountain

forced from the road
by Porsches
mountain horses hide in history
smell different
in pictures

somewhere the Hole in the Head gang
golden youths on horseback
run brumbies eternally
through summer sun

images flicker into black and white
color fades, gone the scents of
horses, dogbush, dust
trailing hoofbeats
laughter, whips

this
thus
then

you're right, that day was perfect
that's where the rot began

-- Mercedes Webb-Pullman

Getting Acquainted

on the first day of pre-school
I push a red sucker
across to the curly-haired boy

he shoves a sticky
green one back

we trade chips and pop
in high-school

he gives me
chocolates
for each anniversary

-- Joanna M. Weston

Placebo

As an artifact of Catholic schools,
I accepted half-truths,
As long as they served the purpose of a good story,
Like some that are in the Bible.
So I had no trouble believing
My friend sitting next to me at lunch.

Even when I knew he was manipulating me to share my M&M's,
The ones the nun gave me for scoring highest on a beatitude test.
He didn't come right out and ask;
He had heard her warning me against charity,
That if I shared them I was just encouraging laziness.

Rather, he took the approach that I would reward him for his tale:
How his Dad's uncle, before World War II,
First came up with the idea of coating bits of chocolate in hard candy.
He had bet that since children love to mimic their parents
They too would love to take pills.

Pharmaceutical firms had recently developed the technology
Of compressing remedies, which had until then been dispensed in packets, into pills.
Why not give kids their own version,
A sign they were growing up, just like candy cigarettes?
But that approach never caught on.

It wasn't until the Army Air Corps
Were supplied with candies in cardboard tubes shaped like bombs,
That the product became successful.
The military wanted its crews to have an extra burst of energy
On their extended missions to bomb and burn
The last cities of the German Empire,
Those left with nobody but children and the infirm.
When the pilots returned home,
And this he heard from his father who was one of them,
They brought with them an appetite for his uncle's invention.

Except for his father.
He once heard his father tell his uncle

It also brought back the flash and smoke of crumbled cities,
That the sound of the candy coating cracking
Reminded him of bones breaking.
Which was why this candy was never allowed in his house.

Feeling sorry for the way his parents were treating him,
I passed him my last three.

-- Ron Yazinski

Retiring

His gnarled hands tug at the fallen tree
removing it from tired years of cold,
blistering winters that freeze the lungs'
warm breath and slows the sap in cottonwoods.
The earth stained his old callous hands
defining the lifeline he made his home.
He grasps the steel handled saw steady as
his handshake. He cuts decayed limbs down to
neat timber— the rotted topsoil breathes again. Green
leaves of rhubarb unfold in the warm sun. *Come get it*
he offers to his numbered visitors.

The lonely coo-coo in the kitchen clock chirps
quietly in the farmhouse. Untouched
candy cements in the clouded blue dish.

-- Jennifer Zidon

From The Editors

I Segregate My Jellybeans

lay them out in anticipatory rainbow
of flavors. I eat them judiciously,
in quantitative order, extricating
colorful stripes of sugared imitation,
fruit effigies in ascending denominations,
saving the group with the largest population
for last.

-- A.J. Huffman

Gummy Bear Sex Ends with ER Visit

The couple was out of their depth at the start.
Man gives woman a giant gummy bear
as a gift? Something bad was bound
to happen. In attempt to make the candy more
than it was, woman gets inspired,
convinces man to try
kinky sex, to eat
this poor gelatinous animal from each other's skin.
The big mistake occurred via microwave
melting of mock mammal.

Like candle wax was the thought process
that had apparently seen a few too many erotic movies,
but the candy did not cool when it touched
her skin. Her chest
was on fire and her hands were tied.
Man's instinct for help was worse
idea of attempting to lick the molten mess.

Both burned in various places, they ended
up with severe sugar burns, and a spot
on an upcoming documentary called *Sex
Sent Me to the E.R.*

When interviewed, the couple said they planned
to have a party when the show airs,
and future sexual encounters that stay
away from all things that might be hot.

-- *A.J. Huffman*

Life is *Like a Box of Chocolates*

the dollar-store-holiday-leftover variety.
Full of undistinguishable crap,
every bite is bitter
and hard to swallow.

                    -- A.J. Huffman

With Slice

of red dye-infused, sugar-dusted gummy
mock fruit sticking to my teeth, I wonder,
momentarily, about the ramifications of
each chewing motion . . .

                            empty calories
collecting on hips, waiting to be cycled
off.

                            future fillings,
enamel erosions, cavities corroding
their way inside back corners.

                            insomnia,
fuelled by temporary saccharine high.
Mind racing, limbs twitching, spastic
muscular tantrums.

. . . The last bit swallowed, faux cherry
flavor lingers, dissipates. I forget myself,
automatically reach for another piece,
comforted by the bizarre repetition of this self-
destructive scene.

                        -- A.J. Huffman

I Would Kill to Lick a Tic Tac

the would-be star said
on national television, and I wanted
to digitally bitch slap some sense into
this walking testimony to stupidity.
This cannot be
the mirror we hold
before our daughters' eyes, this self-
eviscerating image of disintegrating
beauty. This starving
need for attention at any cost
that glitters for a moment,
but, like an oasis, is really nothing at all.

-- A.J. Huffman

Two Jelly

beans were sitting at the dinner table discussing
the relevance of manipulated metaphors
in contemporary fiction
when an apple rolled through, made some snide
sideways remark about their ration (caloric count
vs. nutritional value), flipped
them off before moving on. [Sugar]Shock struck
the duo silent. Suddenly,
they simultaneously burst
into giggling fit. *What a peel!*
Jinx! Their laughter echoed
through dawn.

-- A.J. Huffman

With Lollipop

Lips part in pose of reception.
Glistening red
bulb of sugared satisfaction
approaches. Stick raising flag
of fancy plays peek-a-boo
with salacious tongue. How many
licks does it take to reach restricted
core?

-- A.J. Huffman

Finding the Center

Life is like that—waiting in the bedroom
for someone to confess having
smashed every single one of the chocolates
in the box of assorted creams looking
for that one golden caramel always
in the disguise of a corner, square king,
deceptively hard. You wouldn't know
if you didn't press your index into it.
The answer is always in the last one you touch.

-- April Salzano

Beggar's Booty

Halloween. The old woman,
surrogate mother, taught the toddler
to say she didn't need to beg
door to door for candy. She had
enough. And to prove it, she displayed
her loot—sour patch kids, Reese's cups,
the big ones, and her own tiny boxes
of Milk Duds. Like dolls still in plastic,
and the swimming pool, a circle in shade
of basement, there was no one to share it with.

-- April Salzano

(Lemon)Heads are Gonna Roll

down sloped floor of movie theater
during the best part. If nobody turns
to locate source of disturbance, check
for three unattended adolescents
in the back row, we will just start firing
the three-dollar-a-box jewels like spit wads
at the backs of unsuspecting heads,
one by one. We will not stop until we annoy
them all. It is a duty, a rite of passage.
To fail means nothing less than a life of regret.

-- April Salzano

Peanut Butter Meltaway

disappears, chocolate first, then thick
peanut guts, smooth as ground silk
that can only be called creamy,
if one is concerned with accuracy.
Each perfect square is a secret,
a private joy in an individual
wrapper that stays behind
as morsel is lifted from emptying
box. Guilt makes gluttons of us all.

-- April Salzano

Whatchamacallit

He said I tasted like candy.
What kind? He wouldn't specify,
mainly because he has no imagination.
Metaphor is something for the uselessly
educated, those with low-paying jobs
and high student loan payments. Debt
is something like an Easter egg, full
of surprise, never ending, and if
you don't look, could stay hidden
for years.

-- April Salzano

Fear is

a thin, breakable membrane,
a wait-till-your-father-gets-home
apprehension. A door opened.
Fear is a forgetting that anyone
you don't know includes everyone,
even the man who lives
next door. Fear is the candy
he holds in his fat, eager hands.
Fear is our little secret.
Fear is knowing
he means what he says.

-- April Salzano

How Many Licks Does it Take

to get to the center of a poem?
Here is one
on a stick, hard-shelled exterior,
gooey center like
chocolate-covered saliva, waiting
to be swallowed. Read for the
teeth-marked metaphor,
candy coating in red
or orange, either bitten
straight through or sucked
until a colored tongue wraps
around something solid to consume.

-- April Salzano

Author Bios

Allen Ashley is the author or editor of 10 published books; the most recent being "Astrologica: Stories of the Zodiac" (as editor), which was published by Alchemy Press UK in 2013. He is a well-known figure in the British Fantasy society and is the judge for the BFS Short Story Competition. He runs five creative writing groups including Clockhouse London Writers. He also co-hosts a jazz-poetry event in Enfield, London, England.

Barbara Bald is a retired teacher, educational consultant and free-lance writer. Her poems have been published in a variety of anthologies: *The Other Side of Sorrow, The 2008* and *2010 Poets' Guide to New Hampshire, For Loving Precious Beast, Piscataqua Poems, Of Sun and Sand, The Widow's Handbook* and *In Gilded Frame Anthology.* They have appeared in *The Northern New England Review, Avocet, Off the Coast* and in multiple issues of The Poetry Society of New Hampshire's publication: *The Poets' Touchstone.* Her work has been recognized in both national and local contests including the Rochester Poet Laureate Contest, Lisbon's Fall Festival of Art Contest, Conway Library's Annual Contest, Goodwin Library's Annual Contest, and The Poetry Society of New Hampshire's National and Member Contests. Her recent full-length book is called *Drive-Through Window* and her new chapbook is entitled *Running on Empty.* Barb lives in Alton, NH with her cat Catcher, two Siamese Fighting fish and a tank of Hissing Cockroaches.

James Bell has published two poetry collections *the just vanished place (2008)* and *fishing for beginners (2010)*, both from *tall-lighthouse* in London. Born in Scotland he now lives in France where he contributes articles and photographs to an English language journal and continues to publish poems nationally and internationally with recent print appearances in: *The Journal, Elbow Room, Shearsman, Tears In The Fence, Under The Radar and Upstairs at Du Roc.* His latest eBook is *By Shinkansen to the Deep South (Poetry Super Highway 2013).*

Andrew Campbell-Kearsey is a former headteacher/principal who now writes short stories. His first anthology was printed last year by Spinetinglers, called 'Centurionman.' Two of his stories have been filmed and screened at Cannes and at the Hollyshorts Film Festival, Los Angeles.

Theresa A. Cancro is from Wilmington, Delaware, USA. She is a Pushcart Prize nominee, writes poetry and fiction. Many of her poems have appeared in print and at online sites, including Three Line Poetry, Jellyfish Whispers, Napalm and Novocain, Pyrokinection, Leaves of Ink, The Artistic Muse, The Rainbow Journal, Kumquat Poetry, A Handful of Stones, A Hundred Gourds, Lyrical Passion Poetry, Chrysanthemum, and Shamrock Haiku Journal, among others.

J.R. Carson has multiple prose pieces in publications such as *Anathematic*, *Skive Magazine*, and *Defenestration*, plus poetry on *Mindl[ess] Muse* and in the *Storm Cycle* anthology. An award-winning playwright, his poetry placed at the 2006 Sandhills Writers Conference and garnered him an invitation to Bread Loaf in 2007. In most of his work, he tries to tell at least three different stories from at least five different points of view, or whatever the cosmos may give him.

Alan Catlin has published in many genres for many years. His latest full length book is a memoir with poetry about the deaths of his parents, "Books of the Dead."

Cathleen Chambless is a 2nd year poet obtaining her MFA at Florida International University. She grew up in Miami and proudly works with the Miami Poetry Collective. She also works for the FIU magazine Florida Gulf Stream as a poetry reader. Cathleen is also a visual artist and musician. She incorporates these elements in her poetry.

Oliver Cutshaw has published poetry, short stories, articles, and non-fiction works. He is currently writing a memoir of his father's career as a jockey in the heyday of the horse racing industry. Originally from the East Coast, his works frequently appeared in the literary journals and pop culture weeklies of the Boston area. He now resides in Southern California working as a librarian.

Joseph M. Faria had his first book of short stories "From a Distance" published in June 1998. He has also published a collection of poems "The Way Home", and a children's book "The Polar Bear with Wiskers". His poems or stories have appeared in *NEO, The Rhode Islander, Snowmonkey, Temenos, Riven, Zoetrope All: Story Extra*, and was a Glimmer Train Finalist for 2001 and 2004. He has another collection of stories set to be published in October of 2014. He lives in Cranston, RI with his wife Sandra, and their dog, Josie.

Pattie Flint is an uprooted Seattle native toughing it out in New England and spends her days as an editor at Medusa's Laugh Press specializing in hand-bound books. She has been published in *InkSpeak*, *HESA Inprint*, *Hippocampus* and *TAB*, amongst others. She is currently working on her MFA at Cedar Crest College.

Chris Fradkin is a former beet farmer now living in Brazil. His prose and poetry have appeared in *Monkeybicycle, Thrice Fiction,* and *Thrush Poetry Journal*. His songs have been performed by *Fergie, The Plimsouls,* and *The Flamin' Groovies*. And his Emmy-award-winning sound editorial has graced *The X-Files*.

Phil Ginsburg is a performance/poet whose work can be heard at Indie Feed Poetry Podcast. He has two chapbooks: Psychotropic Poems and The Choreography of Corn. His short play "Another Day in Polka-Topia was the winner of the 2010 Alan Mineri Award at the American Globe Theater in NY.

Jessica Gleason writes because Bukowski no longer can. She likes to break the norms, do some writing, drink some whiskey, and then repeat. Gleason has one published novel, "Madison Murphy, Wisconsin Weirdo" and a new chapbook, released in March 2014 by Popcorn Press, entitled "Sunset on this Town". Her work can also be found in Postcard Shorts, The Idiom, The Writer's Eye, Fickle Muses, Misfits Miscellany, Citizens for Decent Literature and Verse Wisconsin. If you want to read more of her work, Google her. You can find poems, prose and samples of her novel all over the Internet, but you have to work for it. She also, occasionally, likes to sleep in a Star Trek uniform and has mastered The Song of Time on her Ocarina.

John Grochalski is the author of The Noose Doesn't Get Any Looser After You Punch Out (Six Gallery Press 2008), Glass City (Low Ghost Press, 2010), In The Year of Everything Dying (Camel Saloon, 2012), the novel, The Librarian (Six Gallery Press 2013), and the forthcoming collection of poetry, Starting with the Last Name Grochalski (Coleridge Street, 2014). Grochalski currently lives in Brooklyn, New York, where he constantly worries about the high cost of everything.

Lynn-Marie Harper writes poems mainly, sortieing sometimes into stories and enjoys writing daily as self expression and exercising creativity. She has had poems published in anthologies and on a cd. She reads much, works in a library, the sweet store for the mind and arena of all folk. She reads to patients in hospice. Her interests include non-duality, sunshine and flowers, the latter a treasure in England where she lives and thrives mostly in the very capital, very varied city of London, the freedom of which she takes full advantage. She has worked doing many things including teaching dance and working with young people.

William Ogden Haynes is a poet and author of short fiction from Alabama who was born in Michigan and grew up a military brat. His first book of poetry entitled *Points of Interest* appeared in 2012 and a second collection of poetry and short stories *Uncommon Pursuits* was published in 2013. Both are available on Amazon in Kindle and paperback. He has also published over a hundred poems and short stories in literary journals and his work has been anthologized multiple times.

Art Heifetz teaches ESL to refugees in Richmond, Va. He has published nearly 150 poems in 11 countries, winning second prize in the Reuben Rose international competition in Israel. He loves Middle Eastern sweets. See polishedbrasspoems.com for more of his work.

Ruth Holzer has had her poetry appear in journals and anthologies including *Blue Unicorn, California Quarterly, Edison Literary Review,*

Freshwater, Modern Haiku and *Take Five*. Chapbooks, "The First Hundred Years" and "The Solitude of Cities" (Finishing Line Press). Her latest collection, "A Woman Passing," has just been published by Green Fuse Press. Her poems have won national and state awards and received nominations for the Pushcart. She works as an editor and translator.

Liz Hufford publishes poetry, essays, short stories, and articles. Currently her favorite candy is salted carmel dark chocolate fudge made in Flagstaff, Arizona.

S.E. Ingraham is a retired mental health consumer and award-winning poet (1st, 2013 Tom Howard Poetry contest) pens poetry from the 53rd parallel, and has work in both on-line and print journals. She continues to work on chapbooks, non-fiction pieces, and the ubiquitous WIP novel. When not writing, she is uber-grand-parenting, world-travelling with the love of her life, and compulsively straightening public works of art (hence the miniature carpenter's level always at the ready). More of her writing may be found here: http://whenthepenbleeds.blogspot.ca/ and here: http://thepoet-tree-house.blog.ca/

Diane Jackman has had her poetry appear in The Rialto, Outposts, Words-Myth and Story (Happenstance Press). Winner of Liverpool Poetry Festival 2006, Mystery short story competition 2013 and Deddington Festival 2014. Other works include the libretto for "Pinocchio" for the Kings' Singers/LSO, seven children's books and many stories. She has just completed "Old Land" a series of narratives exploring the lightly-buried past of the countryside, and is now walking the lanes, gathering material for her next sequence. She lives in deepest agricultural Norfolk, England.

Leland James is the author of two books of poetry, *Inside Apples* and *This Is the Way the World Ends/This Is the Way the World Ends*. His poems have appeared worldwide in diverse publications which include *The Atlanta Review; The Spoon River Poetry Review; The South Carolina Review*; *New Millennium*

Writings; Aesthetica Magazine; Vallum; Arc;Orbis; HQ Poetry, The Haiku Quarterly; Magma; and many others. Also, his poems have appeared in several anthologies, including the Fish Anthology, *Harlem River Blues*, Ireland; *Voices Israel;* Anderbo Poetry *Haiku Anthology*; USA; and *The Songs of Angels, Thynks Publications, UK*. Leland James was an International Publication Prize winner in the *Atlanta Review* International Poetry Competition *and* runners up for the Fish International, the Welsh Poetry, and The Society of Classical Poets prizes. He received the *Franklin-Christoph Merit Award for Poetry in 2008*. His work has placed or been a finalist in many other competitions including *Spoon River Poetry Review; The South Carolina Review*; *New Millennium Writings*; *Aesthetica* , Morton Marr, *The Southwest Review,* and the *Bridport Prize.* www.lelandjamespoet.com.

Judith Janoo writes poetry in the Northeast Kingdom of Vermont. She's been published in the Puckerbrush Review and the Dartmouth ILEAD anthology. She was a Flash Fiction winner at the Littleton Arts Festival, and was a finalist for the Ralph Nadding Hill Literary Prize.

Mark Allen Jenkins is currently a PhD student in Humanities with a Creative Writing Focus at the University of Texas at Dallas where he serves as Editor-in-Chief for *Reunion: The Dallas Review*. His poetry has appeared in *Memorious, minnesota review, South Dakota Review,* and is forthcoming in *Every River on Earth: Writing from Appalachian Ohio*.

Joyce Kessel has published two chapbooks of poetry: <u>Secret Lives</u> and <u>Describing the Dark</u> (Saddle Road Press, 2013) and her work has appeared in *The Healing Muse, WNY Poets Waging Words for Peace, cell2 soul, spitballmag.org, Nickel City Nights* anthology, and Kind of a Hurricane Press' anthologies: *Backlit Barbie* and *Point Mass* as well as the journal, *Pyrokinection.* An editing member of Earth's Daughters feminist arts periodical, she teaches literature, writing, and interdisciplinary courses at Villa Maria College.

Marla Kessler is embarking on her passion for fiction after publishing business articles related to consulting and economics. Marla has already written two novels (unpublished), but she is looking to refine her style and find her true voice through short fiction. She has been recognized for several pieces of fiction, including "Lipstick," a 400 word piece of flash fiction that reflects her desire to take readers on an emotional journey while leaving them with something to think about later, and the more light-hearted "The Literal Definition of Coffee" included in Kind of Hurricane Press's *Coffee* anthology. Her writing style is faced-paced and usually centers around strong women who need to find strength within themselves. She has been publishing a blog – www.inmarlaswords.com – to help her readers and fellow writers understand her writing process but more interestingly, the inspiration behind it.

Steve Klepetar has received several nominations for the Pushcart Prize and Best of the Net for his work. His latest collection is Return of the Bride of Frankenstein, published by Kind of a Hurricane Press as part of the Barometric Pressures series.

Mark M. Lewis has previously had work published in *The British Fantasy Society Journal*, *Another 100 Horrors*, *Full Fathom Forty*, *Escape Velocity*, *Scheherazade*, *Estronomicon*, *The Nail*, and others. He has also written and performed in pantomimes. He is still working on two novels. Mark is a member of the Clockhouse London Writers. More of Mark's writing can be found at http://syntheticscribe.wordpress.com/

Deborah R. Majors currently resides on 30 country acres in the Florida Panhandle. She is a wife and mother of two grown sons and a member of Panhandle Poets Society. Deborah has had poems and short stories published in various publications and journals, on-line and in print. Besides writing, she loves family gatherings, practical jokes, open mic nights, and a robust cup of tea.

Jacqueline Markowski has had her poetry appear in numerous publications some of which include *Cochlea/The Neovictorian, Permafrost Literary Journal, The Camel Saloon, Pyrokinection,*

Jellyfish Whispers and (forthcoming) The Rainbow Journal. She has been anthologized in "Backlit Barbell", "Storm Cycle" and "Point Mass" (Kind of a Hurricane Press). Her short stories have appeared in *PoundofFlash.com*. She is a Pushcart prize nominee and was awarded first place in poetry at The Sandhills Writers Conference. She is currently working on a compilation of short stories and a collection of poetry.

Grace Maselli is at work on a collection of essays and poems. She studied for seven years in New York City at The Writers Studio founded by American poet and author, Philip Schultz. Her work has appeared in *Cleaver Magazine, Poydras Review, Streetlight Magazine and The Penmen Review. Her poem, My Hair, If I Dare (Or, What the Hair Is Going On?) was recently published as a mini chapbook by Phafours Press, Ottowa, Canada. She lives in North Tampa, FL, with a husband, two kids, two dogs, and a Coronet guinea pig.*

Shirley McClure is the winner of Cork Literary Review's Manuscript Competition 2009, runner-up in the Patrick Kavanagh Poetry Award 2009 and winner of Listowel Writers' Week Originals Poetry Compeition 2014. her début collection, *Who's Counting?* (Bradshaw Books) was published in 2010. She is currently working on her second collection.

Catfish McDaris is most infamous for his chapbook Prying with Jack Micheline and Charles Bukowski. His best readings were in Paris at the Shakespeare and Co. Bookstore and with Jimmy"the ghost of Hendrix"Spencer in NYC on 42nd St. He's done over 20 chaps in the last 25 years. He's been in the New York Quarterly, Slipstream, Pearl, Main St. Rag, Café Review, Chiron Review, Zen Tattoo, Wormwood Review, Great Weather For Media, Silver Birch Press, and Graffiti and been nominated for 15 Pushcarts, Best of Net in 2010 and 2013, he won the Uprising Award in 1999, and won the Flash Fiction Contest judged by the U.S. Poet Laureate in 2009. Catfish McDaris has been published widely. In The Louisiana Review, George Mason Univ.Press, and New Coin from Rhodes Univ. in South Africa. He's recently been translated into French, Polish, Swedish, Arabic, Bengali, Tagalog, and Esperanto.

His 25 years of published material is in the Special Archives Collection at Marquette Univ. in Milwaukee, Wisconsin.

Ron McFarland teaches literature & poetry writing at the University of Idaho. His book manuscript, "A Variable Sense of Things," is currently in search of a publisher.

Matt McGee writes short fiction and poetry in the local library until the staff makes him go home. His collections "The Geneology of Everyone's Horses" and "We Liked You Better When You Was a Whore" are available on Amazon.

Joan McNerney has had her poetry included in numerous literary magazines such as Seven Circle Press, Dinner with the Muse, Blueline, Spectrum, three Bright Spring Press Anthologies and several Kind of A Hurricane Publications. She has been nominated three times for Best of the Net. Poet and Geek recognized her work as their best poem of 2013. Four of her books have been published by fine small literary presses and she has three e-book titles.

Karla Linn Merrifield is an eight-time Pushcart Prize nominee. She has had 400+ poems appear in dozens of publications. Among her ten published books are her latest, *Lithic Scatter and Other Poems* (Mercury Heartlink) and *Attaining Canopy: Amazon Poems* (FootHills Publishing). Visit her blog at http://karlalinn.blogspot.com.

James B. Nicola is the winner of three poetry awards and recipient of one Rhysling and two Pushcart nominations, has published over 450 poems in *Kind of a Hurricane, Atlanta Review, Tar River, Texas Review*, &c. A Yale grad and stage director by profession, his book *Playing the Audience* won a *Choice* Award. First full-length collection: "Manhattan Plaza" scheduled for 2014. https://sites.google.com/site/jamesbnicola

Cristina M. R. Norcross is the author of *Land & Sea: Poetry Inspired by Art* (2007), *The Red Drum* (2008, 2013), *Unsung Love Songs* (2010), *The Lava Storyteller* (2013) and *Living*

Nature's Moments: A Conversation Between Poetry and Photography, with Patricia Bashford (2014). Her works appear in North American/international journals and anthologies. She was the co-editor for the project *One Vision: A Fusion of Art & Poetry in Lake Country* (2009-11) and is currently one of the co-organizers of Random Acts of Poetry & Art Day. Cristina is also the founding editor of the online poetry journal, *Blue Heron Review*. Find out more about this author at: www.FirkinFiction.com.

George H. Northrup is President of the Fresh Meadows Poets in Queens, NY, a Board member of the Society that selects the Nassau County Poet Laureate, former President of the New York State Psychological Association, and currently on the Council of Representatives that governs the American Psychological Association. Recent publications include *Buddhist Poetry Review, First Literary Review—East, Generations, Long Island Quarterly, Moebius, The New York Times, Performance Poets Association Literary Review,* and *Step Away Magazine*. http://www.georgehnorthrup.com/Poetry.html

Vincent O'Connor has been a published writer since fourth grade, when his poem about protozoa was first published. Over the years he has published poetry in various print and online publications, as well as magazine articles, training material for various organizations, technical manuals for software companies, and a play, "Nearly Departed."

Susan Oke spends her days working in the Higher Education sector, and her nights, weekends and every spare minute writing short stories and working on her first novel. Her short stories have appeared in several magazines and anthologies, both in print and online. Susan blogs occasionally for the webzine Astronaut.com, and maintains her own blog at: http://susanmayoke.wordpress.com/

Carl Palmer has no wrist watch, cellphone or Facebook friends. He sleeps late untethered in University Place, WA. Motto: Long Weekends Forever.

Mangal Patel is a semi-retired Director of Information Technology (IT) and a Governor of a school. She is married, has twins and lives in London, UK. Relatively new to writing, her published stories include 'Revolving Lives' (anthology Boscombe Revolution Issue 2, Hesterglock Press), 'Dramatic Encounters' (The Casket), 'Lightening Force' (Wordland3), and 'Thunder Smoke' (The Little Gold Pencil). Her story 'Time's Up' appears in the anthology Tic Toc (Kind Of Hurricane Press).

Richard King Perkins II is a state-sponsored advocate for residents in long-term care facilities. He has a wife, Vickie and a daughter, Sage. He is a three-time Pushcart nominee and a Best of the Net nominee whose work has appeared in hundreds of publications including Poetry Salzburg Review, Bluestem, Emrys Journal, Sierra Nevada Review, Two Thirds North, The Red Cedar Review and December Magazine. He has poems forthcoming in Broad River Review, The William and Mary Review and The Louisiana Review.

David S. Pointer has new work included in "Haiku of the Dead" anthology. His most recent poetry book is entitled "Oncoming Crime Facts" sold at www.lulu.com.

Stephen V. Ramey lives and writes in beautiful New Castle, Pennsylvania, a rust belt city on the verge of renaissance. His work has appeared in various places including Cease, Cows, Gone Lawn, and Zest Literary Magazine. He edits the annual Triangulation anthologies from Parsec Ink as well as the speculative twitterzine, trapeze. Find him at http://www.stephenvramey.com

Edward J. Rielly teaches in the English Department and directs the Writing and Publishing program at Saint Joseph's College of Maine. His most recent books are *To Sadie at 18 Months and Other Poems* (Moon Pie Press), *Legends of American Indian Resistance* (ABC-CLIO), and *The Sister Fidelma Mysteries: Essays on the Historical Novels of Peter Tremayne*. A memoir of his childhood, *Bread Pudding and Other Memories: A Boyhood on the Farm*, is forthcoming.

Zack Rogow is the author, editor, or translator of twenty books or plays. His seventh book of poems, *My Mother and the Ceiling Dancers,* was published by Kattywompus Press. He is the editor of an anthology of poetry of the U.S.A., *The Face of Poetry*, published by University of California Press. Currently he teaches in the low-residency MFA in writing program at the University of Alaska Anchorage and serves as poetry editor of *Catamaran Literary Reader*.

Brad Rose was born and raised in southern California, and lives in Boston. He is a Pushcart Prize nominee, in fiction, and a 2013 recipient of the Camroc Press Review's, Editor's Favorite Poetry Award. Brad's poetry and fiction have appeared in *The Baltimore Review; San Pedro River Review*; *Off the Coast*; *Third Wednesday*; *Boston Literary Magazine; Right Hand Pointing; The Potomac; Santa Fe Literary Review; The Common Line Journal; The Molotov Cocktail; Sleetmagazine; Monkeybicycle; Camroc Press Review; MadHat Lit; Burning Word,* and other publications. Links to his poetry and fiction can be found at: http://bradrosepoetry.blogspot.com/ His chapbook of miniature fiction, "Coyotes Circle the Party Store," can be read at: https://sites.google.com/site/bradroserhpchapbook/ Audio recordings of a selection of Brad's published poetry can be heard at: https://soundcloud.com/bradrose1

Janice D. Rubin is a vocational and career counselor. She received her M.S. in Public Affairs and Community Development from the University of Oregon and her B.A. in English Literature. Her poems have been published in Glass: A Journal of Poetry, Flutter Poetry Journal, Tiger's Eye Poetry Journal, Rattlesnake Review, Arabesques Review and The Quizzical Chair Anthology, She was nominated for the Pushcart Poetry Prize in 2008. Her Chapbook Transcending Damnation Creek Trail and other Poems was published by Flutter Press in 2010.

Len Saculla is based in London , UK , Len was previously published in "Tic Toc". He has also featured in "The BFS Journal", "Wordland", "Unspoken Water", "Crab Tales" and most recently online at Tube Flash at The Casket. Direct link:

http://www.thecasket.co.uk/tubeflash/not-falling-down/ with "Not Falling Down" - a piece of flash fiction based on the London Bridge tube station.

Bobbi Sinha-Morey is a poet living in the peaceful countryside of Colusa, California. Her poetry can be seen in places such as *Plainsongs, Pirene's Fountain, Taproot Literary Review, Open Window Review,* and *Bellowing Ark,* among others. Her books of poetry are available at www.writewordsinc.com, and her website is located at http://bobbisinhamorey.wordpress.org. She is a member of The Academy of American Poets.

Smita Sriwastav is an M.B.B.S. doctor with a passion for poetry and literature. She has always expressed her innermost thoughts and sentiments through the medium of poetry. A feeling of inner tranquility and bliss captures her soul whenever she pens her verse. Nature has been the most inspiring force in molding the shape of her writings. She has published two books and has published poems in journals like the Rusty Nail (Rule of Survival)and Contemporary Literary Review India (spring lingers),four and twenty, Paradise Review, Literary Juice, Blast Furnace and many more and one of her poems "Unsaid Goodbyes" was published in an anthology called 'Inspired by Tagore' published by Sampad and British Council. She has also had a few poems published in the anthology ' A Golden Time for Poetry. She has written poetry all her life and aims to do so forever. Her poetry can also be read online on her blog Rain-Chimes- My Poetry Blog: http://drsmitasriwas280.wordpress.com/.

Marianne Szlyk remembers buying ten-cent Snickers bars at the Minit Mart in Fitchburg, MA. She is now an associate professor of English at Montgomery College, Rockville as well as an associate poetry editor at the Potomac Review. Her poems have appeared in Of Sun and Sand, [Insert Coin Here], Something's Brewing, and Storm Cycle 2013. Other poems have appeared in Jellyfish Whispers, Napalm and Novocain, Aberration Labyrinth, Linden Avenue Poetry Review, Poetry Pacific, The Foliate Oak Literary Journal, The Muse--An International Journal of Poetry, and churches children and daddies. She now has a poetry blog at http://thesongis.blogspot.com/.

Yermiyahu Ahron Taub is the author of four books of poetry, Prayers of a Heretic/Tfiles fun an apikoyres (2013),Uncle Feygele (2011), What Stillness Illuminated/Vos shtilkayt hot baloykhtn (2008), and The Insatiable Psalm (2005). A number of his Yiddish poems were recently set to music by Michał Górczyński and performed at various venues in Warsaw, Poland. Taub was honored by the Museum of Jewish Heritage as one of New York's best emerging Jewish artists and has been nominated three times for a Pushcart Prize and twice for a Best of the Net award. Please visit his web site at www.yataub.net.

David Turnbull is a member of the Clockhouse London group of sci fi, fantasy and horror writers. His most recent short fiction has appeared in Vignettes at the End of the World (Apokrupha) and Black Apples (Belladonna Publishing). More information on his work can be found at http://www.tumsh.co.uk/

Annaliese Wagner graduated from Stephen F. Austin State University with a BFA in creative writing and is now earning an MFA in creative writing from McNeese State University. She has been previously published in *Gingerbread House Literary Magazine* and *Blue Lyra Review*, and is forthcoming in *Weave Magazine*.

Mercedes Webb-Pullman has had her poems and stories appear in many online journals and anthologies, eBooks and in print. She lives on the Kapiti Coast, New Zealand. Visit her website at www.benchpress.co.nz

Joanna M. Weston is married, has two cats, multiple spiders, a herd of deer, and two derelict hen-houses. Her middle-reader, 'Those Blue Shoes', published by Clarity House Press; and poetry, 'A Summer Father', published by Frontenac House of Calgary. Her eBooks found at her blog: http://www.1960willowtree.wordpress.com/

Ron Yazinski is a retired English teacher who, with his wife Jeanne, lives in Winter Garden, Florida. His poems have appeared in many journals, including The Mulberry Poets and Writers Association,

Strong Verse, The Bijou Review, The Edison Literary Review, Jones Av., Chantarelle's Notebook, Centrifugal Eye, amphibi.us, Nefarious Ballerina, The Talon, Amarillo Bay, The Write Room, Pulsar, Sunken Lines, Wilderness House, Blast Furnace, and The Houston Literary Review. He is also the author of the chapbook HOUSES: AN AMERICAN ZODIAC, and two volumes of poetry, SOUTH OF SCRANTON and KARAMAZOV POEMS.

Jennifer Zidon is a poet who lives in Fort Collins, CO with her husband and two daughters. She has been published in two undergraduate publications,*The A Journal* of Colorado State University and *North Country* of the University of North Dakota. She was also a contributor of *Kind of a Hurricane Press's* recent anthology *What's Your Sign?* She enjoys writing and editing poetry and currently is working on her first full manuscript.

About The Editors

A.J. Huffman has published eight solo chapbooks and one joint chapbook through various small presses. She also has two new full-length poetry collections forthcoming, Another Blood Jet (Eldritch Press) and A Few Bullets Short of Home (mgv2>publishing). She is a Pushcart Prize nominee, and her poetry, fiction, and haiku have appeared in hundreds of national and international journals, including Labletter, The James Dickey Review, Bone Orchard, EgoPHobia, Kritya, and Offerta Speciale, in which her work appeared in both English and Italian translation. She is also the founding editor of Kind of a Hurricane Press. www.kindofahurricanepress.com

April Salzano teaches college writing in Pennsylvania where she lives with her husband and two sons. She is currently working on a memoir on raising a child with autism and several collections of poetry. Her work has been twice nominated for a Pushcart Award and has appeared in journals such as *Convergence, Ascent Aspirations, The Camel Saloon, Centrifugal Eye, Deadsnakes, Visceral Uterus, Salome, Poetry Quarterly, Writing Tomorrow* and *Rattle*. Her first chapbook, *The Girl of My Dreams,* is forthcoming in spring, 2015 from Dancing Girl Press. The author serves as co-editor at Kind of a Hurricane Press (www.kindofahurricanepress.com).

Made in the USA
Lexington, KY
31 August 2014